ALSO BY KAT TIMPF

*You Can't Joke About That: Why Everything Is Funny,
Nothing Is Sacred, and We're All in This Together*

I USED TO LIKE TO LIKE YOU UNTIL...

(How Binary Thinking Divides Us)

Kat Timpf

THRESHOLD EDITIONS

New York   London   Toronto   Sydney   New Delhi

Threshold Editions
An Imprint of Simon & Schuster, LLC
1230 Avenue of the Americas
New York, NY 10020

First Threshold Editions hardcover edition September 2024

THRESHOLD EDITIONS and colophon are trademarks of Simon & Schuster, LLC

Simon & Schuster: Celebrating 100 Years of Publishing in 2024

For information about special discounts for bulk purchases, please contact
Simon & Schuster Special Sales at 1-866-506-1949 or business@simonandschuster.com.

The Simon & Schuster Speakers Bureau can bring authors to your live event.
For more information or to book an event, contact the Simon & Schuster Speakers Bureau
at 1-866-248-3049 or visit our website at www.simonspeakers.com.

Interior design by Silverglass

Manufactured in the United States of America

1 3 5 7 9 10 8 6 4 2

Library of Congress Cataloging-in-Publication Data is available.

ISBN 978-1-6680-6727-7
ISBN 978-1-6680-6729-1 (ebook)

*To my dad, who taught me to think for myself, and my husband,
who accepts the market risk of me doing so*

Contents

". . . hate suits him better than forgiveness. Immersed in hate, he doesn't have to do anything; he can be paralyzed, and the rigidity of hatred makes a kind of shelter for him."

—JOHN UPDIKE, *RABBIT RUN*

Introduction

As the meet and greet started wrapping up at the Montgomery, Alabama, stop on my tour, I found myself overwhelmed with guilt. One person toward the end of the line was *so* out of place, I just *knew* that she didn't want to be there.

Why was I so sure? Because she was young, covered in tattoos—including on her neck—and, quite clearly, a lesbian. Her family, all of whom were much older, had definitely forced her to come, probably because they needed a ride or something, and I felt a strong urge to shout out: "Hey, sorry I exist because if I didn't, then you wouldn't have to be here right now."

Her family started asking me lots of questions about *Gutfeld!*, the Fox News show I co-host every day, while she, as I'd expected, hung far, far back. Once her family walked away, however, she did something that I didn't expect: come up to get a photo with me and tell me she had a question of her own.

"Sure, what is it!" I said, smiling on the outside but internally preparing myself for her to ask me what it felt like to be ruining the country.

"You've dated a girl before, right?"

I was stunned. I had been so, so wrong. Well, except about the lesbian part, but you get what I mean.

Not only that this person was there on purpose because she liked me, but also because, you know, yeah, I have dated a girl, and apparently, she somehow knew that, or at least strongly suspected it, because if she didn't, she wouldn't have asked me that. She especially wouldn't have waited until the very, very end, making sure no one was listening but her, if she thought I wouldn't answer the way that I did. Which was, "Yeah," and then some muttering about how almost everyone in my life knew that, but there was nothing about it on the internet, because I always worried that if I were to talk about it publicly, then The Public might turn it into a bigger deal than it was to me, which is that it's no bigger deal than the fact that I've dated men.

She also offered me her number. Although I declined, I didn't mind that she'd offered. A woman flirting just doesn't feel as uncomfortable or offensive or alarming as it does when it's coming from a man. It might not be fair, but there's plenty of unfairness regarding the sexes that tilts in men's favor, stuff like them generally being able to physically overpower most women. Which I am sure is, like, a total coincidence in terms of their advances feeling less comfortable.

Anyway! I am sorry, Montgomery Lesbian in the Red-and-White Air Jordans, that I doubted you . . . but you taught me something about myself. I had just been up onstage preaching about how messed up it is that so many people will notice a single thing about a person and then assume that it tells you everything that you need to know about that person. It's the thesis of this book, which I'd already been writing, and yet, I'd still gone and done it myself. I thought that her being a neck-tatted lesbian meant she didn't want to be here in this room full of old white straights, and was so certain that I'd actually wasted mental energy feeling embarrassed to be in front of her.

Unfortunately, the impulse to allow a single facet of a person to form your overall opinion of them can lead to far worse outcomes than unnecessary embarrassment. All too often, we will let a single difference in viewpoint or association be enough to write off another person entirely, even if we know nothing else about them.

A lot of people have used some variation of the phrase "I used to like you until . . ." on me throughout my life: "I used to like you until you told me how you voted" or "I used to like you until you told that joke" or "I used to like you until you got food coloring all over our apartment from Popsicles that were mine in the first place. I know you apologized, but you posted a YouTube video you made dancing around with them called 'It's Popsicle time, bitch!' just minutes later, which made the apology mean a lot less." (Okay, that last one might have been fair. Sorry, Emilia. I really am.)

There are, of course, many legitimate reasons to write people off. What is *never* a good reason, though, is on behalf of a partisan-political-power scheme that cares nothing for you, other than as a pawn for its own ends. This scheme has, unfortunately, been increasingly successful—blinded by outrage, we're missing the reality that it's rarely if ever as simple as one team versus another. Issues are often nuanced and complex, and people always are.

By the end of this book, you'll be reminded of this reality, and also see how, the more divided and tribal and polarized we become, the more we'll lose. We miss out on opportunities to connect, or even collaborate, all while people in power over us turn us against each other for their own gain.

I begin this book by calling myself out not because it's fun, but because it's important. Throughout this book, in fact, you'll see me be far more vulnerable than an admission that I misjudged a stranger—which is terrifying, but will hopefully show you how vulnerability might be a huge help getting us out of this mess.

LFG.

I
USED
TO LIKE
YOU
UNTIL...

1

I Work in Pornography

In the past, I've told random people at parties (you know, the kind of people you'll literally never see again, but are stuck talking to for three to seven minutes until you can think of some reason you have to go) that I work in porn instead of telling them I work at Fox News . . . because it's less controversial.

I've shared this trick several times, including with *New York Times* reporters who were doing a piece on *Gutfeld!* And do you know what they did? They wrote: "Ms. Timpf—a libertarian commentator who tells friends in New York that she does pornography because, she said, it is 'far less controversial' than naming her employer," which made me sound psychotic and didn't even make sense logistically. I have *friends* who think I fuck on camera for a living? How would that even work? They come to my birthday parties and are like, "Headed to that porn girl's birthday!" and I've managed to keep this ruse up despite being on literal (non-fuck-related) television for a decade?

Other times, I simply say I work "in television" and follow it up immediately with a question about their job, or I just say I'm "a writer." One of my favorite answers to the "What do you do for work?" question is a simple "No thank you!," which usually weirds people out enough to move on to something else.

Dropping the Fox News bomb at a party changes the vibe of the entire thing. People will look around, like, *Who let her in? She's complicit in hatred!* And then pull out their child-labor-built phones to text shit about me to each other. Sometimes someone will say something like: "How can you handle working at a place that's devoid of compassion for the marginalized?" Like, bro, don't you work at a *bank*? (Oddly enough, the announcement of bank employment never leads to "How can you handle working at a place that takes away people's homes?" questions!)

Once I bring up my employment at Fox News, the interaction ceases to be a conversation and instead becomes some kind of weird hybrid between a job interview and a police interrogation, except I'm not constitutionally entitled to a lawyer.

But when I say I work in porn, I'm met with, "Oh, really? That's cool!" Because they don't want to seem judgmental.

As for me, I'm also not judgmental about porn careers. In fact, a whole *career* in porn is objectively impressive statistically speaking; most can't make an entire career out of it. According to a CNBC interview with Steven Hirsch, owner of Vivid Entertainment, the average female porn actress makes only between $800 and $1,000 per sex scene, and someone with "bad representation" might make as little as $300. Although I've never worked in porn, or any kind of sex-related industry, I don't consider it, OnlyFans, or even boots-on-the-ground sex work to be anything other than another person's decision to make, which, of course, is none of my business. I don't even find it scandalizing. Politically, I think it should be decriminalized, because rightfully, in a free society, you own your own body and the government does not. Of course, it's also not something I've been able to bring myself to do, Fox News employee notwithstanding, especially as my dad is still alive. I've put the poor guy through enough already. For example, most dads wouldn't have to know that their son-in-law had sex with their daughter while she had an ileostomy, let alone sit next to him while she talks about it onstage during her live show. I just wouldn't feel comfortable with a video of me having sex living online forever, but I also don't see my lack of comfort with it as a moral high ground. It's just a personal preference that actually comes with a pretty big downside: not making as much money as I would make if I did leave my current life behind to start an OnlyFans instead. Sure, the average creator on that platform may make between only $150 and $180 per month, but I am (unfortunately) the star of enough perverted, pornographic deepfake photos and videos to make it disgustingly clear that there absolutely is a market for my nudity. Not to brag. Or barf.

Anyway! I know what the Public Perception of Fox News is by many of the people who have never walked through the doors of 1211 Avenue of the Americas: It's the channel For Old White Men by Old White Men, a haven of heartless Republican lunatics. I also know, as someone who has worked there for nearly ten years now, just how much that perception differs from the reality of my own experience. Fox News isn't a monolith. Sure, the prime-time lineup is stacked with hard-core conservatives like Sean Hannity, Jesse Watters, and Laura Ingraham. The host of the show I co-host, Greg Gutfeld—although definitely outside of the typical conservative mold as a pro-legalization agnostic with perhaps the most homoerotic sense of humor I've ever encountered—is conservative. But Fox also employs talking heads who are Democrats, like Jessica Tarlov and Harold Ford Jr. It employs meteorologists, makeup artists, camera operators, floor directors, and many others, all of various political persuasions. It employs apolitical anchors, unafraid to ask the tough questions relating to Donald Trump and his administration, like Neil Cavuto and Bret Baier. It employs straight-news reporters like Trey Yingst, whom I've seen countless times calmly reporting from the Middle East as rocket fire rages above him.

Back to Gutfeld for a second: Unlike me, or the people I just mentioned, Gutfeld *is* a Trump guy. We disagree, including on his show,

about several issues, such as stop-and-frisk and broken windows po-
licing (he's pro; I'm anti). And guess what else? We're close friends!
Throughout my time at Fox, I've also gotten close with Dana Perino,
turning to her for advice regarding both my personal and professional
life, although there are certainly areas (Edward Snowden, to name
one!) where we've strongly disagreed politically.

There are lots of ideologically different friendships at Fox. Democrat
Jessica Tarlov is a friend not only of mine but also of Greg's. The three of
us have gotten dinner together after work. We've hung out at his apartment. We've celebrated his birthday. (Notice that I said "his" and not
"ours." Despite my near decade of close friendship with Gutfeld, the guy
has never made it to a single one of my parties.)

The liberals who somehow see my position on Fox News as a tacit
endorsement of every single statement that's ever been uttered on the
channel—as if that would be possible, given the fact that there *is* debate
on our air—don't get it, and the conservative viewers who comment
trash about Tarlov with Greg and me tagged in it, as if we would agree
with calls for her firing because we disagree on economic policy, don't
get it either.

By the way: When it comes to Trump himself, I'm low-key proud
of my ability to thoughtfully consider news related to him on a per-
issue basis. I have a set of core principles, and my view of any situation
depends on those principles instead of a predetermined allegiance. The
partisan lens is so powerful, people from opposing groups can look at
the exact same subject and see something completely different. Like
Trump's mug shot! A Trump supporter would say it's evidence that
we've become a banana republic, and that Trump's arrest threatens the
very existence of our nation. But a Democrat looking at the same photo
would say it proves that *Trump himself* threatens our nation's existence,
and that democracy will not survive if he regains power.

A tender balance, I'm aware, not everyone is capable of. But Ice

Cube was! In October 2020, he announced he'd been working with Trump to help create a plan that would create jobs for black Americans, which both sides interpreted as "Ice Cube Goes MAGA," pissing off the Left and elating the Right. This, even though Ice Cube had posted on then-Twitter, now-X in August 2016 that he would "never endorse a mothafucka like Donald Trump! EVER!!!" and released a song in 2018 called "Arrest the President." Ice Cube was clear in his reasoning for the collaboration, saying he saw it as "a totally bipartisan issue that the country wants to solve." He later explained he'd been speaking with both campaigns, but that Trump's was the only one that wanted to delve into the issue with him before the election. I've always been a fan of Ice Cube. "Once Upon a Time in the Projects" has been one of my favorite songs since childhood (damn, I really have always been a libertarian, haven't I?), and I became an even bigger fan once he declared his defiance of blind partisan loyalty. Sure, he later said he would vote whichever side implemented his agenda, even if it were Trump, but made it clear that this was not because he was taking Trump's side, but because "[e]very side is the Darkside for us here in America. They're all the same until something changes for us. They all lie and they all cheat but we can't afford not to negotiate with whoever is in power or our condition in this country will never change. Our justice is bipartisan."

Ice Cube wasn't declaring a new partisan alliance, he was rejecting the tyranny of partisan alliance, refusing to allow the demands of partisan purity to stop him from helping find solutions to a problem that he cared about.

Unfortunately, Trump was such a lightning rod that you had to unequivocally shun him—even if you thought working with him on something might make the world a better place—to avoid the Blue Team declaring you an irredeemable pariah.

Just as many on the Left will demand that you unequivocally shun Trump for them to consider you an acceptable human being, many on Team MAGA have demanded that you unequivocally support him. Believe me, I've been on the receiving end of just how *not* well some Trump supporters can take it when someone speaks anything but glowingly about him.

As frustrated as I've felt at times, I've also seen plenty of reasons for hope. Throughout my nearly forty-city tour of "You Can't Joke About That LIVE," I saw so many different places in the country, from Portland, Ore., to Jackson, Miss., meeting so many different people along the way. Since this was a show about humanity and connection as opposed to politics and division, I found that, as different as all of us were, we all had even more in common. Another thing I found? How shocked the theater staff was to see my performance, often turning wide-eyed to members of my team and exclaiming: "*She* works at Fox News?!"

It's not that I don't have anything in common with conservatives; that's not the point! I'm a small-*l* libertarian, which means I'm a registered independent who uses the common noun "libertarian" to represent her political philosophy, which is that the government should be limited and questioned and individual rights respected. There are many misconceptions about what this means. For example: Contrary to what many people may think, believing that government power isn't the best way to solve a problem does not equal not caring about the problem. Similarly, focusing on people as individuals doesn't deny the importance of working together. Actually, it demands it! If each of us is a unique individual with unique strengths and weaknesses, then we will need to work together if we want to achieve the best outcomes. But I'll get more into all that later.

In any case, Fox News is the place that's given me a platform to share my own views as a nonpartisan thinker, including the importance of not hating people based on a differing political view or alliance. When I guest-hosted *Gutfeld!* in August 2023, I did a whole monologue about how we must remember that thinking a person's view on a political issue is bad should not equal you thinking that the entire person is. I've talked about the dangers of blind partisan allegiance repeatedly, actually, including on an episode of *Gutfeld!* in March 2023, saying:

> I'm way more interested in conversations at this point about the people versus the system than partisan conversations of Republican versus Democrat . . . I'm not a Republican or a Democrat; I never have been, but . . . it's just become so clear to me that it's more about party than principles, and the one thing that's made that so clear to me lately is the views on the military. I've always been really antiwar; I've always been a huge critic of the military-industrial complex, I think the Department of Defense is more like the "Department of War Makes Money" . . . you can see how many times they've lied to us for . . . [ambition] and money reasons, but that's something in the past that people on the Right would scream at me about . . .

At which point Greg interjected: "That I would scream at you about," before I continued:

> Especially you! And now, people on the Left are screaming at me about it . . . I can sometimes have a conversation with someone that's better who is super Left-wing, for example, than a party-line Democrat . . . because at least they agree that the system and people in power kind of lie to you, and we should be confronting that and be honestly searching for the truth based on principles.

(Note: I have continued to not allow the fog of war to cloud my principles. For example: My first book espoused the importance of free speech and of refusing to weaken the First Amendment, and I've stuck to that, even when anti-Semitism on college campuses was prompting some others who had claimed to be pro–free speech previously to now want to make concessions in that area. In a discussion on *Gutfeld!*, I reiterated my belief that "even the most hateful, vile hate speech is constitutionally protected under the First Amendment," adding that I *still* didn't feel comfortable agreeing to give up our rights for the sake of banning speech, no matter how hurtful we might find it. I added that I remained consistent and firm in my belief that the answer to hurtful speech was using our own speech to counter it, and that "censoring constitutionally protected speech" on campuses was the wrong approach. (I got a lot of *strongly* worded "I used to like you until . . ." comments for that one, even though it was the same thing I was saying when they *did* like me, the only difference being that the speech in question had been something they agreed with.)

Anyway! My comments on that March 2023 show about being a nonpartisan thinker were picked up by stand-up comedian and nonpartisan political commentator Jimmy Dore, who shared them on his radio show, saying he completely agreed with my point, but also adding: "I don't see how she's gonna make it on Fox."

But I've always been free to openly express my views on Fox, even when a segment was clearly framed with the opposite point of view. Just one example: In February 2021, I was invited on Harris Faulkner's show to discuss Dr. Carl Hart, a Columbia professor, psychologist, and neuroscientist, who had admitted to dabbling in heroin. The framing, quite clearly, was that a professor admitting to heroin use was outrageously unacceptable. But since I'm pro-legalization in real life, I'm also pro-legalization on the air. So when Harris asked me for my reaction, I said:

> Honestly, I think the more important thing to talk about rather
> than his heroin use is some of the policy ideas that he's discussing,

which are things that I happen to completely agree with. Personally? I don't do heroin. But the fact that he does heroin also doesn't affect me. He says in this country, we are supposed to have the right to make whatever choices we want to make for our own lives as long as they don't interfere with other people's rights to do the same . . . He also points out the fact that the vast majority of overdose deaths in the United States are from illicit substances, and that a lot of harm could be reduced by legalization and regulation, which is also something that I agree with.

Harris was a bit stunned. Kind of like she would be in an interview a few months later when I'd tell her I'd like to abolish the Bureau of Alcohol, Tobacco, Firearms and Explosives, because most of the agency's attention is on taxation, regulation, and prohibition—very little of it goes toward the investigation and prosecution of violent crimes, and those are things that other agencies can and do handle. She asked me to clarify that I really didn't want to express outrage over Dr. Hart's heroin use: "So, it doesn't bother you that he's talking about that illicit drug use . . . in a way that you know has an outreach to his students?"

I stuck to my guns, explaining that, although heroin can lead to addiction and death, so can alcohol and even food.

I clearly have a different point of view than what many people expect to hear on Fox News. The fact that they don't know they can get multiple views watching the channel highlights an ignorance that goes far beyond just random people at parties. I've had actual journalists make the mistake of seeing that I'm a "Fox News contributor" and assuming that tells them everything there is to know about me. A year or so after that heroin interview—as well as, you know, countless other instances of me saying the same thing, both on air and in my columns—Rafi Schwartz, a writer at the now-defunct millennial news website Mic, published a piece accusing me of "hypocrisy" for saying I was "on board with ayahuasca." Why? My position as a Fox News contributor clearly meant that I must have been anti-drug previously, and the only reason I was saying that I was cool with ayahuasca now was that footballer Aaron Rodgers, whom he called a "Trump-leaning himbo," had admitted to doing it, snarking: "All it took was a Trump-supporting handsome white guy multimillionaire athlete to get the ball rolling." This was not the only time this sort of thing has happened to me, either. In August 2023, TheWrap identified me as a "conservative, traditional, kind of hardcore Right-winger." Yeah, bro. Hard-core Right-wing tradwife; that's me!

The way that hearing "Fox News" breaks people's brains is a symptom of what has *really* broken people's brains, and that is binary thinking . . . if it can even be called "thinking" at all.

I've said it before, and I'll say it again: Binary thinking is the enemy of critical thinking. For some reason, we've largely limited ourselves to just two options on so many crucial, complex issues.

Once you pick a side or a lens, you no longer have to think, because all the thinking has been done for you. No matter the issue, you'll just go with whatever the people on your side are saying. You don't have to challenge your beliefs or feel uncomfortable. Unfortunately, that stunts personal growth, as well as personal relationships that could have been fulfilling.

As an independent, libertarian voter who works at Fox News, I've had to face this issue too many times to count. Some wild things can happen when you've refused to choose a team while working at what just might be *the most hated place* by one of the teams. I've learned so much by doing just that, and I can't think of anyone else in the same position as I am—which means, somehow, I'm the only human who can actually write this book.

After ringing in 2016 co-hosting the Fox News New Year's Eve preshow, I swung by the end of a party at a friend's house, mostly because I knew that her friend, a girl for whom I'd had a thing for years, would be there too.

I USED TO LIKE YOU UNTIL... 11

It went well enough for her to come home with me for the first time ever, and *that* was going so well that she was still over the following night—until her family showed up to collect her from my house. Although I'm sure there was more to it than this, it was a move that our mutual friend would tell me had been inspired in part by the horror of her ultra-feminist, gender-studies-professor mom over the fact that her daughter was with a girl who worked at Fox News. (I know; I'm *such* a fuckin' bad boy!)

For the record, it would turn out to be far from the last time we would see each other. For the next several years, we would go on to have a relationship whose dynamics were so confusing, even to the both of us, that trying to explain the nature of it to anyone first required the question: "How much time do you have?"

Anyway, what happened that night really is the perfect illustration of a major problem with our discourse. I mean, honestly—let's think about how silly that gender-studies-professor mom's fear was, just for a second. I was, uh, definitely *not* being *anti*-woman with her daughter. How could she have freaked out so much over something so clearly illogical?

But the reasoning behind her dismay will never make sense because it probably didn't involve reasoning at all. It was likely a blind reaction to hearing "Fox News," based on the conditioning and demands of her chosen political team, rather than any kind of thought-out response to what was actually happening.

And, like, I don't mean to shade her mom as being uniquely obtuse here, either, because it's not like this sort of thing is uncommon. Unfortunately, knee-jerk reactions based on political conditioning have infiltrated institutions far more influential than my old Bushwick apartment, and with far greater consequences than an early, abrupt ending to time with a girl.

Refusing to interact with people you disagree with, after all, will inevitably lead to you believing incorrect assumptions about them. Believe it or not, supporting the Second Amendment does *not* automatically equate to caring more about guns than children's lives. Rather, it might just be because of a different fear, perhaps of children living in a country where there would be no Second Amendment check against government tyranny. Or get this: Enjoying performing in drag does *not* equate to a desire to groom your kids. Actually, it doesn't even equate to giving enough of a shit about your kids to say hi to them.

And guess what? Someone you might disagree with on guns or gender might be a super valuable relationship to you in some other way. Maybe you each have a parent suffering from the same illness; maybe they love the same sports team; maybe they have a good lawyer that can keep you out of jail. Who knows? But we'll never find out if we keep writing everyone off the way we do now.

Unfortunately, we *do* do that now. Or, as the John Updike quote I picked for the epigraph of this book puts it: ". . . hate suits him better than forgiveness. Immersed in hate, he doesn't have to do anything; he can be paralyzed, and the rigidity of hatred makes a kind of shelter for him."

The idea of hate as a shelter provides an interesting lens to try on when examining partisanship, especially during a time when politics is intensely and increasingly motivated not by common goals, but common enemies.

A 2018 Axios poll found that 61 percent of Democrats viewed Republicans as "racist/bigoted/sexist," and about half of Democrats viewed Republicans as "ignorant" (54 percent) and "spiteful" (44 percent). Similarly, 49 percent of Republicans called Democrats "ignorant," and 54 percent said Democrats were "spiteful." Only 4 percent of respondents believed the other side to be fair; just 3–4 percent said the other side was "thoughtful." Oh, and about a quarter of Democrats (21 percent) and Republicans (23 percent) said they believed that the other side was *evil*—or, in other words, a full 44 percent of the country was walking around in 2018 believing the other side to be not simply people with whom they happened to disagree, but people who were actually *evil*.

Now, presenting politics as a battle between good and evil works great for politicians. It's a message I'll discuss in detail throughout this book: Convincing voters that a vote for you is a vote against evil can be extremely motivating. If you believe it, when you go to vote, you're not just a voter, you're a warrior. You're Batman; you're Superman; you're Frodo in *The Lord of the Rings*. (Having tickets to go see *The Lord of the Rings: The Return of the King* was the only time my mother ever let us leave Mass right after Communion.)

The thrill of feeling morally superior has no doubt played a huge role in how we've gotten to where we are now. In a 2017 study with results so obvious that I'm shocked they conducted it at all, psychologists concluded that moral outrage was often rooted in self-interest rather than altruism. It allowed people to feel less guilty about how they might be contributing to society's problems without them having to do anything to solve them. In fact, the more a person felt guilt over a problem, the more their moral outrage toward a third-party target increased. But it gets worse: The more guilt people felt over possibly being at fault, the more they *wanted to punish* a third party with that outrage—and the greater their opportunity to do this, the better they felt about themselves.

Although lobbing insults at another person might make you feel better, it doesn't mean that you are better, and it's certainly not a way for any of the issues that we face to get better, either. In fact, the way that we keep unfairly and unnecessarily tearing each other apart is making our problems so much worse that I had to write a whole book about how it would be cool if we could cut that out.

As I unpack various issues, it will become clear that a lot of things are nuanced, and people always are. Each of us is varied and unique, and our political and social opinions will reflect that. What's more, it's okay that they do!

The book will also delve into the way that binary thinking enables government corruption. Rather than needing to face any actual account-ability for wrongdoing, each side just points out things that the Other Side did that were "worse," and people in power spend far more time fighting these completely unwinnable and self-righteous arguments than they do looking for actual solutions. They then anticipate that we'll fight *each other* about these things, and can always rest assured they'll have millions defending any of their wrongdoing for the sake of the Good Team.

It's pathetic, but it's true: Politics makes us fight with the people we actually know on behalf of people who don't even know we exist. It would be much better to have good-faith, freethinking conversations. When you think about it, any "conversations" between the Two Sides—where they just shout talking points at each other about how what the Other Side did was worse—don't even really count as conversations at all. They're more along the lines of a childish, schoolyard "I know you are, but what am I?" taunt. Actually, it's the exact inverse of that; it's "*I know I am, but what are you?*"

The way people in power use partisanship and the demonization of The Other to manipulate us and play us against each other will be an overarching theme of this book. They do this on issues ranging from gender and sexuality to war to surveillance to taxation—making it easier for them to get away with growing and abusing their own power, often getting us to agree to give up our own rights in the name of The Team.

Much like how my first book, *You Can't Joke About That*, examined the usually dry and thorny issue of First Amendment rights and free speech in an entertaining and vulnerable way, this book will also be funny and full of fun stories to illustrate all these points. I hope this writing will make it *enjoyable* for people to do the usually hard work of examining their beliefs and biases to challenge power structures and open themselves up to the idea that they might have something in common with another person whom they may have previously written off, or even seen as irredeemable.

This work is essential, not only in terms of the joy and fulfillment that relationships with others can bring us on a personal level, but also on a larger scale, allowing ourselves to be open to hearing and discussing solutions for society's problems from a wider pool of people. If this book does what I think it can, together we will save America—by rejecting reflexive outrage and hatred based on assumptions in favor of thoughtful consideration, real conversation, and hating people only when they really deserve it. I'm not Fox News. I'm Kat, and if you're going to hate something about me, then it might as well be for who I really am.

If at any time reading, you're tempted to think to yourself: "Kat, you work at Fox News, how can you say all this?" It's just like, okay, well, I *do* work at Fox News, and I *am* saying it.

Of course, as soon as this book is announced, I'm sure there will be critics posting things along the lines of: **A FOX NEWS GIRL IS COMING OUT WITH A BOOK ON POLARIZATION?!?!?! LMFAOOOOOOOOOO**. And they will be making a great point! Just not the one they think they're making.

In fact, they'll be making mine.

2

Politically Nonbinary

The very first night I spent in the apartment I'd moved into with my then-boyfriend-now-husband, Cam, I slept between him and one of our friends: a gay democratic socialist who now works as a producer at MSNBC.

He'd spent the day with us drinking White Claws (it was the summer of 2019, and White Claw was really the only hard seltzer around back then; kind of hard to imagine now that each influencer on Instagram seems to be hawking a different one) and unpacking boxes. He lived deep in Brooklyn, so we weren't going to be jerks and make him travel all the way back down there late at night after helping us out just because we didn't have any furniture other than our bed, which was big enough for the three of us and my cat Cheens to watch TV in together, anyway.

I'd met him years earlier smoking cigarettes on a fire escape at a party in Harlem, and his quickly became one of my most cherished friendships—not only because he's so sweet and fun and doesn't snore or take up that much room in a bed, but also because he's one of my favorite people to talk politics with.

You might find this surprising, as "libertarian" and "socialist" are philosophical opposites, except for how they're not, which is that they reject the mental confines of the two-party binary enough to think outside of it. Put another way, people like my friend and I actually *do* share a core principle: that the system as it is, is fundamentally flawed.

I can't really overstate just how similar we are regarding this principle. In fact, the same way I'm always clarifying that I'm a small-*l* libertarian and *not* a member of the Libertarian Party, he clarifies that, although "democratic socialist" best represents his collection of viewpoints, he doesn't spend too much time thinking about where his views fit in terms of political parties because of his overarching lack of faith in our political system in general.

Yes, in so many of our discussions, the exact thing that he sees as the solution (the government) I diagnose as the problem. Even so, our conversations have never turned to ad hominem or yelling or anger or bad faith. Not even once, not even after White Claws, not in many years of friendship. The fact that I can have an easier conversation with him, given our generally opposing views, would seem to suggest that the system is the major divider in and of itself, doesn't it?

Often, people say the issue is that we Need More Moderate Voices, but this relationship would certainly suggest otherwise. I'm not moderate; I'm for very small government. My socialist-leaning friend is for very big government. He's an anti-moderate. Perhaps the issue with communication being so hostile and going nowhere is not being too passionate about the issues, but the passionate defense of a *team*, principles aside. I'm further convinced of this because he is far from the only democratic socialist I've noticed I'm able to speak civilly with.

In April 2015, about a month before I got hired at Fox News, I made my first (and so far only) appearance on Comedy Central, as a guest on *The Nightly Show with Larry Wilmore* to discuss Rand Paul's announcement he'd be entering the presidential race. I'd be discussing this topic as part of a panel with two other guests: comedian Baratunde Thurston and the one and only Sen. Bernie Sanders.

I was sitting in the greenroom before the show for a very long time.

Either that or it *felt* long because I was so nervous, probably both, but anyway, at some point, I got up to approach Sen. Sanders and say hello.

I will never, ever forget what he said to me, a very blond, twenty-six-year-old girl in her very best Forever 21 dress, paired with Payless shoes she'd gotten years ago and refurbished for TV by coloring in the scuffs with a Sharpie marker.

He said: "You're from *National Review*! You're not supposed to like me!"

I laughed, but we wound up finding several issues where we shared common ground—*National Review* or not. We had a lot of agreement, for example, on the war machine, which, to Sanders's credit, is something he has managed to remain consistent on, even after Democrats popularized the beating of war drums in Ukraine. I've admired the consistency of his policy positions, even if his number of homes is less than consistent with his Eat the Rich mentality.

By the way: I was more than just writing at *National Review*; I had formed very meaningful relationships with the people there, especially since my mom died just a few months after they'd hired me, giving me no other option but to can't-speak-or-breathe-sob in front of my new bosses when informing them of her illness pretty early on in the gig. To this day, my heart absolutely swells to think of the love and support then-publisher Jack Fowler and editor-in-chief Rich Lowry showed me during this time, not only in terms of words but also in actions. For example: I refused Lowry's offer for Amtrak points so I could stop schlepping on the bus to go see my dying mother at the hospital in Boston. Then, after a day that I came to work particularly distressed because the bus had broken down on my way back, just hours after she'd been transferred to the ICU, I received an email from Lowry's wife, Vanessa, informing me that their points had been transferred to my account. Fowler didn't simply ask me how my father was doing, he became my dad's friend, and they remain so to this day. It's not only that I have no idea where I'd be without the career stepping stone that working at that magazine provided me, but that I also don't think I would have gotten through my life without the personal support it provided me, either. The magazine's editorial board has absolutely come out with opinions with which I've vehemently disagreed—ones involving war often among them—but all these things are still entirely true. In fact, the big tent approach that *National Review* takes with its writers, although all in some ways conservative, is one of the things I respect about the publication the most.

It's a major theme of this book: Having a certain affiliation, or even a certain view, just doesn't tell you everything you need to know about a person. We would be better off with more independent thinking, but as things stand now, people have a hard time even perceiving it as a possibility. If you criticize Biden, that must mean you're MAGA. If you criticize Trump, then that must mean you're a liberal.

I've experienced just how far people will go in their minds to avoid considering independent thinking as a possibility, lengths that have gone far into the realm of conspiratorial. Countless times, I've seen Fox viewers in the comments or in my Twitter/X mentions theorize that Kat Timpf is a "secret liberal." Like, what are you even talking about? For one thing, if I really were a liberal and trying to keep it a secret, I would probably at least try to not blow my cover by doing things like criticizing Trump or, you know, explicitly stating, "I'm not a Republican," the way that I have. How can you consider this weird conspiracy (seriously, what would I be gaining in their minds by being "a secret liberal"?) before considering the possibility that my views just might not fit into the two-party binary? Because things have gone bananas, that's how.

It seems even more bananas to me when I consider how the two-party system, especially the rabidly partisan one that we have now, can lead to a lot of bad outcomes. I know, I know—a lot of people see elections as a binary choice, and vote for what they see as the "lesser of two evils," but for me? I refuse to vote for a candidate who denies my rights or the rights of others, because I see that as being complicit. If you don't recognize and respect my rights, then I'm not going to vote for you to have power over me. Simple. Also, since I think the two-party system in itself creates so much harm, it actually feels good to vote against it. Also also, I live in fucking *New York*, which is, you know, not exactly a swing state.

I get a lot of shit for this, obviously. The fun thing about being a libertarian/independent is, no matter who wins, the team who doesn't will blame you for their candidate's loss. I get it all the time: "Kat, you whine about Joe Biden, but you wasted your vote, so you're part of the problem!" I had a now-former friend shame me in front of others for having then–Libertarian candidate Jo Jorgenson on my comedy-advice show, *Sincerely, Kat*, in September 2020 because *Should I really be giving any platform to other candidates "right now"*? "Right now," of course, intended to mean the time when Trump must be defeated above all else. I have greater respect for people who stick to their principles, unafraid to criticize anyone on any side or to point out flaws in the system. I'll always have an easier time having a conversation with someone whose principles might not align with mine—even when it's someone as close to an opposite as a socialist—than someone for whom principles don't matter as much as partisan alliance. Do those even count as "principles" at all?

As I mentioned in the last chapter, these types of interactions are less conversations than they are a perpetual volleying of "I know I am, but what are you."

It can go something like this:

It is so messed up how Joe Biden said he was not involved in his son Hunter's business dealings, and now it is coming out that Hunter called him twenty times during business meetings!

Oh yeah? Well, Trump was convicted of thirty-four felony counts and is facing even more!

Well, why hasn't Joe Biden been charged, especially since it also came out that Biden sent thousands of emails using fake names, sometimes to discuss Hunter's business dealings!

Well, Trump used fake names too!

Well, that was just to brag about himself to reporters! Biden was using his position of power to make money for his son!

Oh yeah? Well, Trump used his position of power to try to over-throw the election! Jan. 6 almost dismantled our democracy!

Oh yeah? If you hate riots so much, why aren't you upset about the riots in the summer of 2020 that cost billions in damages!

You *would* smear all black people as rioters, you racist!

You hate the police! If someone tries to kill you, I'd better not see you calling the cops!

And so on and so forth. Or rather, not forth. It doesn't go forth; it doesn't go anywhere. It's a pathetic replacement for actual discourse, and it's happening constantly between people on each side. People are not examining or even listening to what the other person is saying; they're too busy thinking about what they can throw back that will show the other person how much worse their side is regardless.

Think, for example, of the first week of August 2023: Trump was in-dicted on four counts related to the 2020 election, and news broke that Hunter Biden put then-VP Joe on the phone more than twenty times during business dinners.

Republicans screamed about the alleged Biden corruption and also about the fact that the Trump indictment happened just one day after the Biden news dropped, insisting it had been timed that way on purpose to distract from the alleged corruption of Hunter and Joe. Meanwhile, Democrats screamed that this Trump indictment was, as House Minority Leader Hakeem Jeffries and Senate Majority Leader Chuck Schumer put it in a joint statement, "the most serious and most consequential thus far."

And the views on all this stuff, by the way, were pretty much divided down the line according to the teams.

An Associated Press-NORC Center for Public Affairs Research poll found that 85 percent of Democrats approved of the charges filed against Trump on August 2, compared to just 47 percent of independents and a measly 16 percent of Republicans. A CNN poll conducted that same month found that, "[e]ven among Democratic-aligned voters who say they'd prefer to see their party nominate someone different in next year's presidential election, just 37% believe Joe Biden was involved in his son's business dealings, and only 29% find his actions regarding the investigation inappropriate"— compared to 76 percent and 90 percent of Republicans respectively.

The one thing each side had in common was what they were screaming about the other: *How do they keep getting away with this?*

Regardless of the specific person or specific charge, it's obvious that being a person in a position of power makes it a lot easier for you to get away with things the rest of us would never be able to get away with.

But to an extent, "the rest of us" help people in power get away with things by being rabidly defensive of politicians for the sake of partisan loyalty. It's not hard to figure out how this works: If politicians have a whole team warding off criticism regarding anything they do, handling it only by pointing out how something the Other Team did was so much worse, then it's obviously going to be easier for them to get away with more. They already have the huge advantages of political power and PR machines, let's not give them the benefit of our simping for them, too.

Yes, I said "simping." You guys know about simps, at least in the usual sense of the word. There are internet trolls, and then there are their opposites, which are the simps. Instead of commenting mean things on someone's post, simps comment nonstop thirsty things. The ones who are like, "Kat, you are the most beautiful and smart woman ever. If I were just forty years younger . . ." (Like, then . . . what? *Then* what would you do, Gerry? Does your wife know you're on here?)

Sometimes, the trolls and the simps argue with each other in the comments. If a troll says something like, "How is she gonna have all that forehead and still be dumb AF," a simp will rush to defend my honor and reply with something like, "She is so smart and beautiful, why are you coming on Kat's page and leaving hate?" and then the troll will hit the simp for being a simp, saying: "Hope she sees this, bro."

To anyone who has ever defended me in my comments, I really do appreciate it. You definitely have better things to do, just like I have better things to do than read them, but I appreciate it nonetheless. I don't mean to smear you guys as simps, because not all of you are simps. Some of you are just fans and not weird about it at all.

(Of course, some of you are *very* weird. For example, the guy who refers to himself as "Captain Save a Hoe," who brought a red, fuzzy BDSM dog leash and collar to my meet and greet in Cincinnati, and then, weeks later, traveled all the way to my Houston show to meet and greet me again. Although I've met him twice, I still don't really know what "Captain Save a Hoe" even means. Am I the hoe? Unclear.)

Anyway, some of the trolls calling other people simps very well may be simps themselves—because partisan politics can indeed turn people into *total* simps for the politicians and candidates on their team.

Whenever I see people post passionate, glowing comments about a politician, or someone viciously attacking the character of a civilian for having posted something supportive of a candidate on the other side, my brain immediately goes: "Hope [s]he sees this, bro!"

It really grosses me out, because being a simp for a politician is far, far worse than being a simp for a celebrity in countless ways.

For one thing, most of these politicians aren't even *a little bit* hot.

For another, the consequences of simping for a politician are far greater than simping for a celebrity. As I mentioned earlier, it makes it easier for people in power to get away with doing corrupt things. But that isn't the only pitfall.

For example: Passionate love for a politician—and, by extension, hatred for his or her opponents—can tear people apart. I said this earlier, but it bears repeating: Politics does an excellent job of making people argue with people they actually know on behalf of people who have no idea they even exist. If that sounds pathetic to you? You're right. Simping generally is.

A Siena College and *New York Times* poll released in October 2022 found that nearly one in five Americans reported that arguments over politics had harmed friend or family relationships. It can also keep them from ever even beginning: Findings from the Survey Center on American Life released in January 2023 found that roughly two-thirds of both liberals and conservatives would be less likely to date someone on the other political team.

It also seems that many political simps might also do what so many of my simps do regarding my marriage: get upset about another person's relationship. A September 2020 Economist/YouGov survey, after all, found that 38 percent of people from both political parties would be upset if their kid married someone from the other one.

Partisan anger—which is, of course, always paired with partisan gloating by the Other Side—also makes for one hell of a distraction. The same week as those competing Biden vs. Trump corruption stories (actually, so close in terms of timing that Axios described it as "[n]early simultaneously with the indictment being filed"), Fitch Ratings downgraded the U.S. credit rating, a move that one of Fitch's senior directors, Richard Francis, blamed on factors including the debt ceiling, "the deterioration in governance," and political polarization. He told Reuters: "You have the debt ceiling, you have Jan. 6. Clearly, if you look at polarization with both parties . . . the Democrats have gone further left and Republicans further right, so the middle is kind of falling apart basically."

Of course, this news got barely any coverage. For one thing, it was boring, especially when there was so much scandalous bad news about the figureheads of the two teams coming out for people to seize on. Like, let's be real. What's more fun: Learning the ins and outs of global financial markets, or posting about how the Walls Are Closing In on the leader of the Other Team, especially as the Other Team is saying the same about your guy?

During this week and in the weeks that followed, while I was working on a cable news network that was reporting heavily on the Biden news—just as heavily, I'm sure, as liberal cable news networks did when it came to Trump's—I was also traveling around the country for my tour. Several times on the road, I would be talking about the way that the system divides and distracts us as it gains its own power (yes, this is the kind of stuff you'll have to hear if you hang out with me; I am often intolerable to be around), only to have someone within earshot *jump in and agree with me*. This happened countless times, and the people who jumped in could not have been more different: a Lyft driver in St. Louis, who would later pivot the conversation to one about how he really thinks Nelly and Ashanti are in it for the long haul this time (I agree); a hairstylist in Cincinnati, who would later pivot the conversation to her children and what it was like to go on a cruise with her girls without them . . . just chitchatting about the failures of the system with near strangers, in conversations that were both effortless and empathetic.

Touring through nearly forty cities taught me a lot about this country, myself, and some of my own biases—like the one I called myself out for in the introduction of this book—but most of all, it's taught me just how much more all of us have in common as humans than the binary thinking and partisanship would make us believe that we do.

To be clear: Partisanship *does* make partisans see the Other Side as enemies simply because they're on the Other Side. That Siena College/ *NYT* poll I mentioned earlier? It also found that a majority of each party's voters saw the other one as a "major threat to democracy." A Pew Research study published in August 2022 found that "increasingly, Republicans and Democrats view not just the opposing party but also the *people* in that party in a negative light," finding that "[g]rowing shares in each party now describe those in the other party as more closed-minded, dishonest, immoral and unintelligent than other Americans." It said: "In 2016, about half of Republicans (47%) and slightly more than a third of Democrats

(35%) said those in the other party were a lot or somewhat more immoral than other Americans. Today, 72% of Republicans regard Democrats as more immoral, and 63% of Democrats say the same about Republicans."

Considering this, it's really no surprise we see people simping for their candidates so hard—if you see people on the Other Side not simply as people with whom you disagree, but as people who are *immoral*, then it's easy to see why you would stop at nothing to defend your own or to take down someone from the other. And *listening* to the Other Side? Please. Everyone knows not to listen to or even be around someone immoral. Everything from the Bible to the elephant graveyard scene in *The Lion King* will tell you how dire the consequences of *that* can be.

As James Davenport, the associate dean for social sciences at Rose State College, wrote in a piece in August 2023 for NonDoc, Democrats and Republicans are "increasingly separating from one another geographically, religiously, and economically," which has "led to significant misunderstanding of our political opponents," including a "perception gap" between the parties that hugely overestimates the number of people in the other party who actually "hold 'extreme' views."

A study released in 2019 on this "perception gap" found similar results relating to extremism: Overall, both Democrats and Republicans "imagine almost twice as many of their political opponents . . . hold views they consider 'extreme'" than they actually do. For example: When Democrats were asked how many Republicans would agree with the statement "Properly controlled immigration can be good for America," there was a 33 percent gap between their guess and the reality. It also worked in the reverse: When Republicans were asked how many Democrats they believed would *disagree* with the statement "The U.S. should have completely open borders," *they* were off by 33 percent.

It makes all the sense in the world, doesn't it? After all, refusing to even associate with people from the Other Side also means that you're operating off nothing but assumptions about them, and our assumptions are wrong all the time. What's more, this perception-reality disparity applies to more than just viewpoints; it applies regarding other characteristics, too: A 2018 study by Douglas J. Ahler and Gaurav Sood found that "people tend to considerably overestimate the extent to which party supporters belong to party-stereotypical groups." For example: People believed 32 percent of Democrats are LGBT (when it's actually just 6 percent) and that 38 percent of Republicans earn more than $250,000 per year (when it's really only 2 percent). What's more, the numbers were even more off when people were estimating about the people in the opposite party: Democrats guessed that 44 percent of Republicans earned more than $250,000, and Republicans guessed that 38 percent of Democrats were gay, lesbian, or bisexual.

If we actually get to know each other, though, we might find that our values align in more ways than we might think.

A survey published in the summer of 2023 by Starts With Us, an organization that seeks to overcome political division, found that, although about 9 out of 10 Democrats and Republicans agreed on the importance of core values like personal responsibility, fairness, and compassion, only about a third from each group said they believed the other side thought those things were important.

I get the temptation of the latter, of course. For example, I can admit that my brain immediately goes: "How can you say you value personal responsibility and be anything but a libertarian?" I also get that these are Unprecedented Times, and that in such times, correspondingly unprecedented anger and fear are to be expected. For example: I'm writing these next few paragraphs as a last-minute addition, on the last day of my final round of edits, the absolute last time I'll be allowed to change anything in this book, just days after the former president and current Republican nominee was convicted on thirty-four felony counts.

Because of the way book deadlines work, I have no idea what's going to happen between now and this book's release regarding Trump, or regarding anything else. But here's the thing: No matter what happens, the message of this book still stands. Actually, it's more than that: I'm not publishing a book about unity and getting along *despite* an environment of consequential political stakes, but precisely *because* of it.

Put another way: I don't know what's going to happen on Election Day, other than the fact that the election won't be the only thing I'm thinking about—as November 5, 2024, *also* marks the ten-year anniversary of the death of my mother: a milestone so striking, it seems impossible to me even as I write it. And guess what? I won't be the only person in this country with something else on my mind on that day, either.

Yep. Even as the election may *seem* to be the only thing worth considering on November 5, that won't be the case for a lot of people out there—and for many, it won't be the case in ways far more significant than the anniversary date of a past tragedy. Again, it may not seem that way when we look around us, but that's all the more reason why we should remind ourselves of it as much as we can.

Thankfully, I'm *very* aware that we share so much more in common than politicians and the media want us to think that we do, and of how much we can lose if we fail to keep that in mind.

I know that I personally would have lost a lot if I couldn't see things that way. Sure, in some ways, it's been tough for me to not have a team, because I get shit from people on both sides, but that's nothing compared to the ways that it's been awesome. For one thing, given the number of libertarians, choosing to surround myself with only people who agree with me wouldn't leave me with too many options for friends. Political stripes of all colors were present at my 2021 wedding. Some of my friends who partied in the streets when Biden won in 2020 were instrumental in helping me get through the most traumatic breakup of my life. (Keep reading if you want the tea on that one.) Some of my friends who celebrated Trump's win in 2016 were vital in helping me get through my emergency ileostomy operation. The friend who allowed me to lower her Uber rating by plugging my phone into the driver's radio and singing "Get Down on It" at the top of my lungs any time we were in the car together, for an entire summer? A conservative. The friend who gave me the cold, hard truth about her bad reaction to a terrible boyfriend of mine in the middle of a party? A progressive. The friend who has given me some of the best career advice, one of the staunchest Republicans you've ever met. The first friend I told about my engagement, a Democrat. The examples are endless.

Personally, every ounce of hatred I've experienced, and every ounce of a lack of belonging I've felt for not having a team, all have been nothing compared to what I've gained from having the ability to enjoy close personal relationships with those who view politics and government differently than I do.

The problem with binary thinking isn't only that it shuts us off from each other personally, or that it allows the government to get away with corruption, but that it can shut us off from being open to solutions or help from people just because of their political team. It's more than just the things we lose as individuals; we're also losing as a society by being hesitant to come together and hear each other out. If we did, if we could just realize that a political label or difference of opinion on one issue was no reason to discount a person on everything, we could solve so many of our problems—or, at the very least, come together and agree to stop bowing the knee to the ruling class, which routinely abuses partisan loyalties and plays us against one another for the sake of gaining and maintaining its own power and control.

Of course, I understand that the politicians we elect do have an impact on our lives. But the preoccupation with partisan fighting distracts us from the fact that there's a much better approach to quelling these concerns.

To me, there is far too much focus on which specific people we will put into positions of power, and not enough focus on the amount of power that those positions have.

Put another way? We wouldn't *have* to freak out about what might happen if This Guy or That Guy got elected if the people we elected didn't have so much authority over us in the first place.

3

Quit Pretending to Be More of a Problem

About a month before I started dating Cam, the rapper I'd been hanging out with (we had said, "I love you," and he'd met my family, but it was *casual*) for a few years posted a picture of me wearing his sweats in his hotel room on his Instagram story.

I knew he was taking the picture, and I knew he was posting it. In fact, his whole reason for doing it was *specifically because* I'd been giving him shit about his flakiness.

And then, almost as quickly as he'd put it up, he took it down. He was quite obviously worried about his image—that his fans would get upset about him posting a "Fox News Girl" like *that*—and I suspect he'd already received quite a few messages from those fans (read: complete and total strangers) saying something to this effect. Liking (or, more precisely, liking-liking) a Fox News Girl would be terrible for his brand, which, I'm sure, he worried might have impact reaching beyond a few DMs and into the realm of affecting his ability to make money.

But guess what? He did like me. I'll spare you the details, but he liked me a *lot*. I also don't want anyone to walk away from this story thinking I'm talking about a guy who's a bad dude, because I certainly don't see him that way. I know he eventually did regret the way he treated me, or at least he told me he did, and in any case, I'll always have a soft spot for him. He was the first person who made me feel okay about some of my more boisterous and ambitious qualities, ones my abusive ex had made me feel like I had to hide because he said they made me intolerable. Actually, Rapper Guy made me feel more than just "okay" about them; he loved those things about me, which went a long way in helping me be cool with myself again. So, I'm still rooting for him, and I'm sure I always will.

After all, it's not like we spent all that time together over the years because we *didn't* get along. Of course we did! We talked about our careers, and we got vulnerable about our demons. Hell, we even mused about division. I was with him the morning of Donald Trump's inauguration! As I left to catch the train to Washington, D.C., to film something for work, he contemplated aloud how, although so many people were devastated over Trump's win, and I was only going to D.C. because I was getting paid to go, there were many other people who'd woken up that morning really, really, really thrilled that it was all happening. They were heading to D.C. for the event all excited, probably talking to each other about how it was "gonna be lit!" (Don't worry . . . "lit" was his word, not mine.)

Basically? Our brands may not have aligned in the eyes of The Public, but we totally did align in another way: as *people*. This isn't unthinkable. The only unthinkable thing is how much of our public discourse pretends it is.

I can't count the times someone has privately told me they like me and/or my work, but refuse to follow me on social media, like my posts, or have me as a guest on their podcasts "because you work for Fox News." So many people have reached out to tell me they agree with me, or they think I'm funny, or they share similar life experiences, or they, too, are sick of binary thinking . . . but add that they worry any sort of association with me might destroy their own careers or relationships. Yes, they're prohibitively concerned that liking one of my *jokes* on Instagram that *aren't even about politics* might lead to the decimation of their entire careers. Several of them are very famous, people you definitely know, who keep me as their shameful little secret.

Every time I hear this, it always sucks. It can be hurtful to learn, for example, that my good friend's longtime boyfriend, a Hollywood director whom I considered so close a friend that I invited him to my tiny, COVID-era wedding ceremony when many other friends' partners (and actually, even many friends) didn't make the list, wouldn't even *send my friend the pictures* he'd taken of the two of us on the Santa Monica Pier one summer out of fear that she might (gasp!) post them. And then people would know that his girl had shared air with me, which might negatively impact his career. Never mind that Fox News is actually not some kind of airborne virus, and if it were, we were outside, which would have greatly reduced the odds of transmission anyway. She told me this only after they broke up, and it really, really hurt me and had me rethinking every single one of our very many hangouts. He'd always seemed to enjoy my company, and laughed at my jokes. I eventually reached the conclusion that the reason I thought we were cool was because, well, we *were*. He wasn't pretending to be cool with me, what he was pretending was that he wasn't. It kind of reminds me of that one guy in high school who liked to make out with me in the hallway after he got out of basketball practice and I got out of mock trial practice, sometimes shoving my hand down his pants, but never acknowledging me during school hours in front of anyone.

It's not like all of this is zero-sum, or that the only downside here is my own stupid little feelings being hurt. Honestly? I wouldn't be surprised if at least one reason so many people have become more radically partisan is that they feel like they have no other choice. *If everyone sees me as XYZ, I might as well be it!* There have been times when I've complained to people about how frustrating the misconceptions of me are, and they've replied by suggesting something along the lines of: *Kat, these people are going to shun you because of your workplace no matter what you say or do anyway . . . why not just go all in?* "Go all in," of course, meaning, make myself as desirable as possible to the Conservative Audience, since that's the audience that generally watches my platform.

The mistake people make in suggesting this, though, is assuming that I let how much I think the people listening will like me just totally dictate what I say. I get the assumption, seeing as my entire career is kind of based on me saying things. Or, as my finance bro husband puts it: "Kat, you take market risk every time you open your mouth." (At least my job is easier to understand than his. When I try to ask him how his day was, and then he tells me, it's basically a race to see how long I can pretend to stay interested. Something with charts and graphs and models and Q1, Q2, Q3, Q4 and wearing a headset.)

Of course, that's not to say that I don't make *any* professional considerations when it comes to what I say on the air. For example, I don't say "shit" or "fuck" on live TV. There's also the consideration of tone. *Gutfeld!* is supposed to be more lighthearted and comedic than other shows on the network. Serious topics are sometimes part of it, sure, but even so, that intended tone remains relevant. This means that sometimes, for example, if a guest is saying something I don't agree with, I'm not going to jump in and interrupt them and spout off statistics to show how wrong they are, the way that I might if it were a different kind of show. And yes, there are *some* differences based on the anticipated audience. For example: If you're trying to persuade someone of something, you should try to make your argument in a way that they'll be open to considering it. Or, there's the fact that *Gutfeld!* is on later at night, so, the way I might discuss Jeffrey Toobin's infamous Zoom call on that show would be completely inappropriate for a discussion of the exact same topic on *The Faulkner Focus* at 11 a.m. That's not a hypothetical scenario; I once discussed this exact topic on these exact shows within twelve hours of each other. After getting makeup done the morning of the *Focus*, a producer called me to make sure I knew that, unlike on *Gutfeld!*, I couldn't refer to it as "jerking off" on a morning show. (I did know.)

That was a wild story though, wasn't it? Or, as I said on Twitter/X at the time:

Women in the Zoom Era: Hi! I'm sorry, I know I look so crazy right now. No makeup and my hair is kind of a mess. Lockdown has been crazy; don't judge me haha. How are you?

Man in the Zoom Era: I'm sorry I didn't check to see if my camera was on before jerking off in the meeting.

Anyway! Among all the things I consider when it comes to my appearances on TV, one that I'd *never* consider would be saying something I don't actually believe. I've never seen the point of having a platform for the sake of having a platform. Money, I guess? I have enough trouble sleeping at night. (And that's an understatement. I mean, imagine not having insomnia. You just . . . sleep? When you want to? Wild. I have *so* much trouble sleeping, and then it gets worse when I start to freak out about how it's so late and I still can't sleep. I know every medical organization and its mother is trying to be helpful when stressing the importance of getting seven to nine hours of sleep a night, but it is so, *so* not helpful for those of us who are well aware, wide awake, and trying. The last thing you need when you can't fall asleep is to think about everything you've ever read about how important it is for you to fall asleep *right the fuck now*. I will be lying there like, "I have twenty minutes to fall asleep or else I am going to have a weakened immune system and then I'm going to get sick and then I'm not going to be able to get everything done that I need to get done and . . ." What, just me?)

Anyway, back to how I'd never consider saying something I didn't actually believe, because there's also this: As hard as it can be to read hateful comments, I can't imagine how much harder it would be to read them knowing that I was getting all that hate for saying something I didn't even think was true anyway.

Of course, all those people who have cautioned me that many will publicly shun me no matter what I say—even if they privately agree with things I've said!—are totally correct. I learn of more examples of them every day. I recently had a friend tell me about his hilariously ironic experience at a party: Throughout the night, individual attendees kept coming up to him and privately whispering that they loved his friend Kat on TV, but begged him to please not bring it up in front of everyone else, because they didn't want to be judged for it. This book will be part of my attempt to bring this stuff to light. Not just so people can finally feel confident enough to admit that they agree with a lot of (or even just some) of the things I share on Fox News's airwaves, but so I can expose the hypocrisy and dangers that come with everything needing to be black-or-white to avoid excommunication from the tribe.

Basically, many people feel that they have to stick with their team's preapproved narratives, or else they risk excommunication. So, even when they might have an opinion—or even a friend!—outside of their team's binary, they're often too afraid to share it. It's a vicious cycle, where the expectation of partisan reactions fuels partisanship even further. All too often, because of nothing but optics, we purposely limit whom we will work with, even as there's so much for us to work *on*.

It's truly nuts because most artists—yeah, even rappers!—will have fans of varying views. Rapper Guy should know that better than anyone. I can admit it; he already knows it: I had been listening to his music for years, and had even paid for a ticket to go to one of his shows, before I slid into his DMs, which is how we met.

Regardless of what the parasocial bonds you've built up in your brain tell you, I'm sure I'm not the only case here. To be clear, I *don't* think that the main reason I've been able to have so many close relationships outside of the conservative world is because I'm libertarian/independent and not conservative. Rather, I have ideologically diverse relationships (again, including many with people who *are* quite conservative) because, well, I choose to value having them. I jump at the chance to get to know a person rather than blindly accept what I'm told I'm supposed to feel. I put myself out there; I'm curious, and a lot of the time, that's really all it takes to build what those who don't bother taking those steps might see as an "unlikely" relationship. In other words, I don't want anyone to walk away from this book thinking that the only reason I've had any acceptance (even if it *is* a secret, private acceptance) among mainstream or nonconservative figures is because I'm not conservative myself. Throughout my nearly ten years spent working at Fox News, after all, I've learned just how many people who work here, even people who *are* very conservative, have these same sorts of connections, too.

Unfortunately, the risk of censure in those cases is a legitimate concern; people do tend to freak out regarding an association with Fox News. The place that I know as a workplace that has given me a platform to freely speak my mind and even to promote this book, and where I've met and pleasantly conversed with people of many varying ideological perspectives, other people see as radioactive. First of all, to be clear, "a platform" is exactly what Fox News is. It's not an idea in itself, but a platform to share them. And yet? "Fox News Bad" is a rabid sentiment you can see clearly when looking at, for example, the Twitter/X mentions of Glenn Greenwald, a Pulitzer Prize–winning journalist who's been consistently antiwar, anti–security state, and pro–civil liberties, getting attacked as some kind of traitor or (*gasp!*) Right-winger for simply appearing as a guest on the channel. Again, Greenwald was simply using the platform of Fox News to share *the exact same* antiwar, anti–security state, and pro–civil liberties viewpoint that he'd always held. Still, you will see him pervasively and viciously criticized because "Fox News Bad"—a criticism that's far too pervasive when you consider how senseless it really is.

Years ago, I was sitting outside having dinner and drinks on the Upper West Side with a friend when a random guy came up to me, at first acting like he wanted a picture with me or something, but then said something to me along the lines of: *How does it feel to be ruining the country?* I know. Who knew I had that much power! I asked him what specifically I'd said that had upset him so much. And guess what? He had no answer.

Just quickly, while we're on this: I also have a hard time with people completely writing off another human being over a single errant comment. I won't get into that too much here, because it's already a major theme of *You Can't Joke About That*, and if you want to hear more, you should pick up a copy. But whenever I see a public pile-on toward a fellow television personality, it always makes me wonder how many of the people piling on could manage to speak extemporaneously on live television for hours and hours per week for years and years without accidentally saying something errant themselves.

As for the guy who interrupted my dinner, though, it wasn't about anything specific I'd said or done. He just knew my face as a Fox News Face, and for him that was enough to warrant accusations of country-ruining. For many people, I think it really is as simple as 1980s anti-drug propaganda: "Just say no to Fox News!" "Fox News . . . not even once!" Unlike in the case of drugs, however, the strategy seems to have been fairly successful in getting people to stop thinking any further when it comes to "Fox News."

But as with anything, the best choice comes from doing a cost-benefit analysis. In the case of drugs, it might be something like weighing how fun you think it would be to try crack against the possible risk of spending the rest of your life addicted to crack. (I've always chosen no crack. To be fair, I've never been offered any, but I can be sure that if I were, I'd conclude it wasn't worth it.)

When it comes to Fox News, or any platform, really, the cost-benefit calculation would look something like this: Will there be harm from me appearing on the platform, and if so, does it outweigh the potential benefits of reaching millions of people regarding something that's important to me?

It's a calculation that I know Greenwald has made because he—often fruitlessly, unfortunately—aims to explain it to his critics, asking questions of them on Twitter/X such as "Which principles do I espouse that are contradicted by my appearing on Fox News?" and following up with "I frequently appeared on CNN and MSNBC without changing topics to condemn them for all their views I found repugnant. Could you answer what I asked?"

As I've already explained in my first chapter, it's simply not true that Fox News is strictly a conservative echo chamber where only conservative people share their strictly conservative views. Somehow, the same people who characterize it this way don't seem to realize that, even if you combined every single comment from every single Right-winger on *The Five*'s Instagram page that's said something along the lines of, for example, *Can't stand lib Tarlov! Get lib Tarlov's lib ass off the show!*, it still wouldn't even come close to what their own side is doing, whether actively or passively, to ensure that it actually does become a conservative echo chamber. Think about it: If every non-Republican listened to your demands that they not appear on the channel, then your grandparents who leave the TV on Fox all day would *never* hear from a Democrat, independent, or libertarian. Do you really think that's a win?

When you're not thinking things through, you can end up not even realizing what you're demanding or wind up being angry without even really knowing why. Or, like Rapper Guy, you could end up perpetuating a trend of misplaced anger by keeping up a ruse that you, too, have boycotted a person—when you haven't even boycotted her from your bed.

Perhaps the bare minimum of what people could do to stop being part of this problem would be to stop pretending to be a bigger part of the problem than they really are . . . and it seems that this advice could be helpful to more than just a few people.

I mentioned this in my last book, but in case you don't have *You Can't Joke About That* memorized, I'll include it again here: A 2022 study by Populace, a public opinion think tank, found that there are huge gaps between what people say they believe and what they actually believe, with the study's summary stating:

> The pressure to misrepresent our private views—to offer answers on politically and socially sensitive questions that are out of sync with our true beliefs—is pervasive in society today.
>
> Across all demographics, every subgroup had multiple issues with at least a double-digit gap between public and private opinion.

Got that? *Every demographic* is largely lying about how they really feel regarding "multiple issues," because they're concerned the truth would cause backlash. Honestly, I can't help but feel as though this fear is probably a lot stronger given the strength of the backlash that they might expect to face by looking around at what's happened to other people. In our society, after all, we see people being entirely dismissed over a single point of disagreement, or a comment that came out the wrong way.

Populace's study wasn't the only one to find a gap between true and public beliefs. A July 2020 Cato Institute study found that almost two-thirds of Americans agreed that "the political climate these days prevents them from saying things they believe because others might find them offensive."

The consequences of society-wide gaps between what people say they believe and what they actually believe are clear: They create, as Populace puts it, "false consensus in the public narrative" that can "drive false polarization, erode trust, and hold back social progress."

There's also this: Across demographic groups, "Hispanics and Independents have the greatest number of sensitive topics with double-digit gaps between public and private opinion (14 out of 25 issues, although what constitutes 'sensitive' is not identical for the groups). In contrast, the groups that have the fewest topics with such gaps are Republicans and Democrats (4 of 25)." I can't claim to know what Hispanics are thinking and why, because, well, I'm not one, but the difference between independents and partisans seems to suggest that people feel a lot more comfortable sharing their views when those views are cemented into a major party's platform. I can't help but think that knowing they'll have the backing of everyone in that party might be a huge part in where their security to speak comes from.

But not everyone feels that they belong. A Pew Research study released in October 2023 found that 37 percent of Americans overall "wish there were more political parties to choose from." It was an even larger share among younger people: 46 percent of those ages thirty to forty-nine, and 48 percent of adults younger than age thirty. About a quarter of people say that having more political parties "would make it easier to solve problems," another number that hiked way up (39 percent) when talking about people ages eighteen through twenty-nine. What's more, another Pew Research study, released a month prior, found "a record number of Americans (28 percent) now expressing unfavorable views of *both* parties."

That's kind of shocking, isn't it? I mean, 37 percent overall is far from most people, but just looking around, you'd probably guess that the number was even smaller.

Honestly, it seems like our estimates of each other are off a lot of the time: A study published in *Nature Human Behaviour* in 2023 found that social media users overestimated the severity of "moral outrage felt by individuals and groups," believing that the authors of certain posts were more upset about an issue than the authors themselves told the researchers that they were, thereby "inflating beliefs about intergroup hostility." They found that this misperception was worse among people "who spent more time on social media to learn about politics."

Worse, multiple studies have shown that simply jiggering social media algorithms to combat polarization does not have the intended effect. A massive 2018 study paid Twitter users to follow a bot that retweeted politicians and media and thinkers from the other side. The result? Conservatives became *way more* conservative, and liberals became a little more liberal. Yeah . . . it managed to make things worse.

This wasn't the only study with these sorts of counterintuitive results, either. In 2023, technology writer Elizabeth Nolan Brown published a piece in *Reason* covering several of them, ultimately concluding that changing algorithms or feeds "can't overcome deeper issues in American politics—including parties animated more by hate and fear of the other side than ideas of their own."

Of course, it makes sense to *want* to blame big tech, and not just because it's low-key infuriating that Mark Zuckerberg managed to become a billionaire despite having the charisma of a bag of milk in a black hoodie. I think that we blame them not *in spite of* the fact that they're seemingly untouchable, but precisely because they are. Think about it: If polarization is all *their* fault, then that absolves us of worrying about what kinds of steps we could potentially take to heal, both among and within ourselves.

In any case, it doesn't really surprise me that tweaks in algorithms didn't do much to change people's minds, because there's really no replacement for IRL interactions when you're trying to get a grasp on another person's humanity, which is much easier to ignore when the only contact is screen-to-screen. I think it helps to get to know actual people, and to approach those interactions with a mindset that's open to learning something, even if that means admitting you were wrong.

You do need to actively choose that mindset, though, because it probably won't come naturally. It requires setting that intention, and then actively checking in with yourself. It's human, after all, to notice patterns and draw connections; biases are human. The best we can do is to acknowledge that, and to remind ourselves that none of us are exempt from believing what might turn out to be a misconception about another person. It might prevent you from, for example, replying to someone who's criticized Trump and saying that they have "Trump Derangement Syndrome," or to a person who has just criticized Biden and saying they must be in the "MAGA cult," when really, they're just one of the 37 percent of politically dissatisfied people in that Pew Research study I cited earlier who "wish there were more political parties to choose from."

To be fair, it does seem like when it comes to the phrase "wish there were more political parties to choose from," "wish" is the operative word. Although there technically are other parties, they're not taken seriously by our political system, and people notice that. The same survey found that just 7 percent called it "very likely" that an independent would win the presidency within the next twenty-five years. Unlike the statistics relating to wishes, there were "only modest differences in these views by age and party."

I can admit that I feel the exact same way myself, even though, again, every single vote I've ever cast, I've cast for a third-party candidate. Perhaps this is why, despite how many people say that they crave more choices, the vast, vast, vast majority of them, if they do vote, still end up choosing from one of the two major-party candidates anyway.

A common criticism of voting for third-party candidates, in fact, is that since they Have No Chance anyway, voting for them is a waste. (As I mentioned in my "Politically Nonbinary" chapter, I disagree with this thinking.) Another common criticism is that these third-party candidates are somewhat of a joke, pointing to, for example, then–Libertarian candidate Gary Johnson's 2016 "Aleppo" flub.

For those of you who don't remember it, an MSNBC panelist asked Johnson what he would do as president "about Aleppo," referring to the Syrian city at the center of the crisis that was dominating the news at the time.

Johnson's answer?

"What is Aleppo?"

Shudder.

Look, it *was* bad. I didn't say otherwise then, and I'm not saying otherwise now. Not knowing the word, after all, suggests that this presidential candidate hadn't read even a single thing about the ongoing crisis. Still, as I also said at the time, if his mistake really had been "disqualifying," as so many people were saying that it was, then literally no one could ever qualify. For one, no one can know everything. For another, although major parties may produce the best politicians, being the best politician is very different from being the smartest person, or the best-read person, or the person with the best ideas.

It's not like the guy who ended up winning, as in Trump, knew everything that was going on in the news all the time, either. In fact, as I pointed out in a column about the flub for *National Review*, Trump had had an exchange with Michael Wolff of the *Hollywood Reporter* a few months prior to Johnson's "Aleppo" flub that went like this:

Wolff: "And Brexit? Your position?"
Trump: "Huh?"
Wolff: "Brexit."
Trump: "Hmm."

Once Wolff told Trump what "Brexit" was—and only then—did Trump answer his question, making it seem likely that Trump had just been buying himself some time with those verbal pauses until he could figure it out, even though Brexit was also dominating the headlines at that time.

The main thing Johnson did "wrong," honestly, *wasn't* not knowing something, but being honest and transparent about that fact. Trump is very skilled in these sorts of situations, so if he had gotten that "Aleppo" question and didn't know the answer, he would have handled it much better than Johnson. Perhaps by confidently declaring: *"When I become President, I will get the best people on Aleppo."*

(To be clear, I'm not saying Libertarian Party candidates aren't ever embarrassing, because they definitely can be. But, as I explained before: When I've voted for those candidates, I haven't been voting *for them* so much as for a system where whoever gets voted in won't matter so much, because those positions wouldn't have the power to so intimately interfere with our lives in the first place.)

Anyway! I actually also think it is kind of good when people, especially politicians and people in media, admit that they just straight-up don't know something. Propping up fake versions of people, after all, means that a lot of us are getting angry for fake reasons. Unfortunately, people almost never pull a Gary, which is part of the reason that it went so viral. The fact that it *did* go so viral, by the way, also means that it might have been the only thing that a lot of people wound up even hearing about him, which is a pretty big bummer for the guy. There's always so much more to know about anyone than the stupidest they've ever sounded!

Another thing that might turn people away from considering a third-party candidate could be that many of them have very little, if any, understanding of what those parties even stand for. Now, I'm not saying that there isn't infighting in the Libertarian Party. There is, and a lot of it is also very dumb. (One of the top posts of all time on the r/Libertarian Reddit page is, "If both parties are consenting adults, would you support the right to 'duel'?" More than 21,000 upvotes and counting.) For one thing, libertarianism by definition prioritizes individual sovereignty, so I'm sure I'm far from the only one who makes sure to designate herself as a "libertarian" with a small *l*, as opposed to the proper noun "Libertarian," to make it clear that I use "libertarian" only as an adjective to describe my view of the role of government, and *not* to indicate that I'm beholden to *that* party, either. (Hell, I'm probably not even the only one who brings that up as often as I've been bringing that up in this book!) To me, the philosophy that the word represents is simple: Individuals have the right to choose to do whatever it is that they want to do, unless it interferes with someone else's right to do the same. (Or, as I've explained it before, "Free markets and no judgies.")

Not everyone understands what the word means. Think, for example, of former CIA director John Brennan, who said in an interview with MSNBC in January 2021 that Biden's intelligence officers were "moving in laser-like fashion to try to uncover as much as they can about" a pro-Trump "insurgency," which is "an unholy alliance" of "religious extremists, authoritarians, fascists, bigots, racists, nativists, even libertarians," calling this a "serious and insidious threat."

During the interview, the MSNBC anchor just moved on to another question, as if claiming an alliance between fascists and libertarians wasn't something that deserved more examination. But of course, it did. The idea of a libertarian-fascist alliance is ridiculous, as the definition of fascism is a belief system that "exalts nation and often race above the individual and that stands for a centralized autocratic government headed by a dictatorial leader, severe economic and social regimentation, and forcible suppression of opposition," while libertarianism "takes individual liberty to be the primary political value."

(Also? Trump is not a libertarian. Also-also? If "religious extremists, authoritarians, fascists, bigots, racists, nativists, even libertarians" *do* have anything in common, it's that every single one of them is free to believe whatever the hell it is that they want to believe without government punishment. Also-also-also? By failing, as Northeastern University public policy professor and political violence expert Max Abrahms put it, to "distinguish between those who use extreme tactics and those with whom he disagrees politically," and seeming to suggest that "both are enemies worthy not only of contempt, but action or at least government scrutiny," Brennan is the one who comes off sounding authoritarian. Just saying!)

Of course, getting angry about an ideology you don't understand is only one manifestation of this problem—remember all those studies I cited in the previous chapter regarding how *off* many people are regarding others' beliefs and identities? I didn't do all that research for no reason, bro!

Basically, what I'm asking for here is for people to stop pretending. We have too many problems already; we don't need to be perpetuating fake ones, too. By doing so, all we're doing is creating a bunch of rules for society that don't even represent what we really want. So, instead, let's be honest—whether that's in admitting that you *don't* know enough about a subject (or person) to be outraged, or admitting that you *do* know a person well enough to like them, regardless of any potential controversial association.

4

Everything Is So Political!

In 2023, I made jokes involving the Holocaust, Hitler, breast cancer, death, religion . . . and yet, my biggest controversy by far came after I joked that country singer Jason Aldean looks like every guy ever to sit at the bar at a Buffalo Wild Wings.

The backlash ranged from verbal abuse, demands for my firing, calls to ban me from Texas, to one confident declaration from some lady named Jill that I "crossed the line" and "alienated 90% of Americans."

Although I'm not so sure where Jill got her "90%" figure from, her comment had been just one of hundreds, if not thousands, of comments like it. I don't know how many there were in total because I eventually decided to stay off social media entirely. I did not have the option, however, to stop checking my email, which, unfortunately, included several messages from a guy saying he would no longer watch *Gutfeld!* because of what I'd said. Or, in his words: **Used to love your subdued humor and commentary on Gutfeld; however, your comments tonight about Jason Aldean's song "Small Town" were over the top from a perspective of an ignorant fucking bitch who obviously isn't in to current issues. Fuck you as I will now not watch Gutfeld whenever you are on, which is all the time, so thanks for contribution to NewsMax, dumb ass. BTW: you used to look better as a blonde with the fake glasses. Up yours, Jack.**

(Note: Before you, in your mind, tell yourself that "Jack" is just some basement-dwelling bumpkin, he used his actual email address, allowing me to search and find out that, actually, Jack is a *doctor*. An "internist" in Kentucky.)

Anyway, we'd been talking about Aldean because his song "Try That in a Small Town" had ignited a massive controversy. The song included lyrics like "Cuss out a cop, spit in his face / Stomp on the flag and light it up / Yeah, ya think you're tough // Well, try that in a small town," featuring imagery including fiery riots, a carjacking, and a man robbing a store with a gun. There was some footage of the 2020 "Black Lives Matter" protests, which Aldean later had removed. The courthouse he filmed himself singing in front of had also apparently been the location where a black teenager was lynched in 1927, history Aldean said he had been unaware of.

Critics on the Left accused him of glorifying gun violence, with many calling the song "pro-lynching." Some country radio stations pulled the song. In response, the Right assembled to heap praise upon Aldean, clearly determined to counter the Left's condemnation with equally rabid adulation.

By the time it was my turn to talk about it on *Gutfeld!*, the story had already been featured pretty much nonstop on the channel all day. Knowing this, and recognizing that the tone of *Gutfeld!* is intended to be more lighthearted, humorous, and creative, a contrast from the straight-news-and-analysis shows—and also *never* deigning to represent myself as someone who thought modern country was good music—I worked at crafting something unique and fun to say that took all of that into account.

Here were the remarks I wound up with:

"I don't like country music, new country music. I love Merle Haggard . . . I don't like new country music, and it sucks that our world sucks so much that that's gonna be, like, some kind of *political statement* that I think this song sucks. I don't know who this guy is, I had to look him up, because, obviously, this story is everywhere. He looks to me like every dude ever who I've seen sitting at the bar at a Buffalo Wild Wings"—at which people in the crowd laughed, and I looked at them and added, "Right? If you put a picture of, like, all the Buffalo Wild Wings regulars, and then him, I don't think I could pick [him] out of a photo lineup. So . . . it's ridiculous to say this is like a pro-lynching song or whatever, but I just want to go back [to] when I [could] say 'This song sucks because new country music sounds like every other new country music song, it all sounds exactly the same, I don't like it 'cause it sucks, not because it's pro-lynching.' And there are some bad things about living in a small town. He does not address that. Like, everything closes early. There's no DoorDash. You think I need a cheeseburger now, wait 'til I had to make it myself."

I knew my job here was to offer something fresh and fun, so I tried to do that, all while pointing out what I saw as a flaw in our discourse: that partisanship was essentially limiting our ability to say anything but one of two things. Of course, I explicitly mentioned feeling like I couldn't make a joke about Aldean without it getting misconstrued as a political statement because I did realize that such a reaction was possible. But I also thought, since I had been so explicit in saying that I didn't intend for my joke to be taken that way, people might, you know, *not take it that way*. In any case, I definitely didn't anticipate the reaction to be as intense as it was.

What I could have anticipated, though, was how well the whole thing worked out for Aldean: "Try That in a Small Town" became his very first No. 1 hit.

Nothing guarantees wall-to-wall coverage, after all, quite like a controversy, and all that airtime is free advertising. I don't know Jason Aldean (if I haven't made that clear enough by now), but I wouldn't be surprised if he knew what he was doing here. Sure, he claimed in an interview with the *Los Angeles Times* that he was "a little surprised" by all the backlash, but I'm not so sure . . . especially considering something else he said: "I felt like the song would probably start a conversation about the state of the country."

And indeed it did! Republican politicians (or, perhaps more accurately, members of their staffs) rushed to their keyboards to pen impassioned defenses of Aldean for social media. Donald Trump even weighed in, writing on Truth Social, in part: "Support Jason all the way. MAGA!!!"

"Every issue can be branded by a political group like a corporation brands their product," Doug Spencer, associate dean for Faculty Affairs and Research at the University of Colorado Boulder, told the school's alumni publication, *Coloradoan*, in March 2023.

The discussion of the song had been so firmly branded as a strictly one-side-or-the-other politically partisan one—"Saying Bad Things About Aldean" equaling "Liberal Team," and "Saying Good Things About Aldean" equaling "Conservative Team"—that my explicitly apolitical commentary wound up getting burned with the mark of it. Why *can't* I just say I think a song sucks without getting labeled with an entire political identity? Whether the source material of my joke was political or not, my joke wasn't. The absurdness of the reaction, considering what I'd actually said, is comparable to someone wearing pink to a Fourth of July party, joking that red, white, and blue aren't her colors, ending up accused of treason.

Also? Although "Try That in a Small Town" was obviously intentionally political, the exact same sort of controversy could have ensued even if it hadn't been, and the song had just been about, say, the joy of raising chickens, with a music video limited to footage of a henhouse.

It's as sad as it is true. I could easily see a chicken-focused song becoming a debate between Right (lauding it as an ode to the value of a family-focused farm life, in opposition to those terrible metropolitan Leftists who want public schools to have your children baptized into the Church of Drag by disciples of RuPaul) and Left (slamming it as an oppressive, archaic anthem that wants to take us back to a time before black people had rights and women could vote).

Political branding can take on such a life of its own that an issue ends up being discussed in a way that's separate from reality. Although I was eviscerated for being up-front about my own metropolitan, DoorDash-ordering lifestyle, it didn't seem to matter to the mob that many, if not most, of the Republican politicians tweeting about the song don't exactly live in small towns themselves, either. Actually, Aldean himself grew up *not* in a small town, but in one of the largest cities in Georgia. My opinion on the song was also enough for me to be smeared as an out-of-touch elitist, even though it is not I, but Aldean, who owns a $10.2 million oceanfront mansion in Florida.

Actually, not stopping to think about the reality of a situation is exactly how so many of our discussions become so senselessly partisan, even when it so obviously would make sense to talk about them in another way. The best example, to me, would be one that the piece in the *Coloradoan* raises as well: environmental issues. As it stands now, the viewpoint choices on environmental issues seem to be only two: Catastrophizing Alarmist Moron (Left) and Ignorant Jerk (Right). On climate, the Left has branded itself as the team that cares about the planet, casting Republicans as either too stupid to recognize science or too greedy to care. The Right has branded itself as the team that cares about the economy, casting the Left as a bunch of elitist scaremonger loonies.

But does this binary framing fit with the facts? I mean, one of the only things that we have in common on this planet is that we all live here. Don't you think that all of us like clean air and water? Don't you think that none of us want to doom our descendants to the horrors of a fiery extinction? What's more, don't you think that all of us also see the value in economic prosperity, and would prefer it to economic destitution?

As the *Coloradoan* notes, it wasn't until fairly recently that environ-mental issues became so partisan, citing Matt Burgess, an environmental studies assistant professor with an interest in combatting polarization.

In fact, a January 2024 report coauthored by Burgess claims that "the fractions of U.S. adults worrying 'a great deal' or 'a fair amount' were nearly identical among Democrats, Republicans, and Independents in 1989."

It may seem incomprehensible now, but we even saw agreement in terms of environmental spending: The General Social Survey in 1990 found that 75 percent of self-described liberals *and* conservatives said that they thought that U.S. spending on the environment was "too little."

Things didn't become split, the *Colorodoan* argues, until Repub-licans refused to ratify the Kyoto Protocol, a pledge to reduce green-house gas emissions by 150 countries in 1997, on the grounds that it would hurt the U.S. economy, along with concerns that it would put an unfair strain on the United States that other countries would not have to bear. (An argument that *was* fair, and still applies to this day. Looking at you, China, India, and Russia.)

Here's the thing, though: If you go back to the Two Sides of the 1997 Kyoto Protocol, there are many reasons to see both sides as right. For example: It *would* be better, in a perfect, simple world, to just, like, stop emitting greenhouse gases.

The problem, of course, is that it's *not* that simple; concerns about economic losses *are* valid. Nothing that any environmental leader could possibly say in their conferences (that many of them fly to on private fucking jets, I might add) about how terrible greenhouse gases are could ever change this reality. A Pew study from November 2019 found that 90 percent of "liberal Democrats . . . think climate policies either help or have no effect on the economy," but an analysis of the economic impacts of limiting the rise of the Earth's temperature to 1.5 degrees by oft-cited climate economist Richard Tol found that the costs of doing so would outweigh any financial benefits, in terms of global annual GDP.

Sometimes, two things can be true at once, and this case is clearly one where the two opposing sides shouldn't be so opposed at all. Don't all of us want clean air *and* economic prosperity? Of course we do. That should be obvious. But, as usual, politics can prevent us from acknowledging the obvious. Unfortunately, a single comment about your concern for the health of the planet will almost certainly place you, in the mind of anyone listening, into the Left camp, and a comment about economic concerns into the Right camp.

What's more, as is the case with so many of the issues I'm discussing in this book, as polarized as we are, we're actually less polarized than The Discourse would make it seem. For example, although there are certainly wide partisan differences in considering climate change "a major threat to the country's well-being"—78 percent of Democrats, compared to 23 percent of Republicans, according to an August 2023 Pew Research poll—Yale Climate Opinion Maps 2023 found that only 16 percent of Americans don't "believe global warming is happening" at all.

There's a huge difference between not considering something "a major threat" and not believing it exists at all—so huge, perhaps, that only something as blinding as rabidly partisan politicization could get us to ignore it.

This hurts everyone—Right, Left, and Other.

For a 2019 *Forbes* piece, Michael Shellenberger, an author and journalist who focuses on environmental and climate issues, talked to Australian climate scientist Tom Wigley and MIT climate scientist Kerry Emanuel, both of whom explained that political extremism is making it a lot harder to find solutions to environmental issues.

"You've got to come up with some kind of middle ground where you do reasonable things to mitigate the risk and try at the same time to lift people out of poverty and make them more resilient," Emanuel said. "We shouldn't be forced to choose between lifting people out of poverty and doing something for the climate."

No shade to Emanuel, but you low-key don't have to go to MIT to see how this is true: When any large group of voices automatically and unequivocally shuts out such a large group of other voices, we essentially eliminate the possibility of ever working together on an issue that requires us to do exactly that.

This seems and is obvious, but I unfortunately don't see Our Discourse changing anytime soon. The Two Sides don't do this for no reason; no one does anything for no reason.

Environmental issues, after all, are extremely complicated. Rather than dive into the nuances of it and weigh each factor against economic and geopolitical concerns, it's much easier to just throw your brain into one of two boxes and just call it a fuckin' day, man.

To see another possible motivator, follow the money . . . a phrase I'm sure you've heard before. In fact, it might be one of those things that we hear so often that we stop thoughtfully considering it when we do. Kind of like when your spouse shouts "Love you!" while rushing out the door to go to work. In many cases, money might easily explain why the partisan sides appear to be so "devoted" to certain causes, or at least to branding themselves as such. Now, I'm not saying that it's impossible for a politician to actually care about an issue, just that there certainly are incentives to pretend that they do even if they don't. According to the latest (2024) numbers from the aptly named opensecrets.org, which tracks the money political parties received from various industries and interest groups, Democrats received a vast majority of the funds from categories including abortion rights (99.9 percent), women's issues (92 percent), education (87.4 percent), TV/movies/music (82.9 percent), foreign policy (88.3 percent), and, yes, the environment (91.5 percent). Republicans received the vast majority of the funds from categories including gun rights (99 percent), oil and gas (87.4 percent), mining (91.8 percent), building materials (88.3 percent), trucking (82.3 percent), and automotive (74.5 percent).

Sometimes, politicians will call this out, but usually only regarding the Other Side. For example, Democrats will call out Republicans for all the cash they get from the oil and gas industry, using language like "bought and paid for!" while completely ignoring that they get virtually all of the funds from the opposite side. And back and forth forever, Amen! Very rarely do we see a politician divert from what's expected of the side they're on, and what happened to former Republican congressman Justin Amash in 2020 might be one reason why. (Full disclosure: Justin has become a friend of mine, a friendship forged by each of us seeing the other subjected to many of the same partisan-and-affiliation-rooted misconceptions, due to our openly existing as nonpartisan thinkers in the hyperpartisan political and media sectors.) Amash broke with the Republican Party in declaring his belief that then-President Trump had committed impeachable offenses in the spring of 2019. He renounced his membership in the party and declared himself an independent just months later on July 4, and cast his vote in favor of Trump's impeachment in December. By January 2020, he'd become a leper in the eyes of donor groups that had once heralded him, *despite not even having changed his views regarding the specific causes that these groups purportedly championed.* As I wrote in a piece for *National Review* at the time: "Although Amash remains *the most* fiscally conservative member of Congress, his departure from the Republican party and support of impeachment have apparently made him a leper in the eyes of the exact same groups who claim to want to fight for fiscal responsibility." For example: FreedomWorks, which had given Amash a Freedom Fighter award for every single one of his earlier eight years in Congress for his "fight for individual liberty and fiscal responsibility," now said it wouldn't support him at all anymore. Club for Growth, which heralded itself on its own website as "the only organization that is willing and able to take on any Member of Congress on policy who fails to uphold basic economic conservative principles . . . regardless of party," and had previously been Amash's biggest campaign contributor, made the same decision, as did the DeVos family and Americans for Prosperity. (Note: Amash did later decide to run for Michigan's open Senate seat as a Republican in 2024, but he explicitly stated that this did not represent any deviation from his viewpoint or values, saying, "What we need is not a rubber stamp for either party, but an independent-minded senator prepared to challenge anyone and everyone on the people's behalf.")

Of course, this issue goes far beyond just politicians and their donors. Whenever money is a factor, it has to be considered as such, which is why I am always so suspicious of corporations Taking Up a Cause. To me, it seems pretty clear that they seek to brand themselves as champions of certain causes because they want to attract consumers, and not because they actually care. Perhaps one of the most newsworthy examples in recent years would be Bud Light and Dylan Mulvaney. In case you've been living under a rock, Bud Light sent a single specially designed can to Mulvaney, a transgender influencer, with her face on it to celebrate the one-year mark of Mulvaney beginning her transition, reportedly paying her to post with the can in April 2023. Conservatives had a meltdown about Bud Light Going Woke, and the beer's parent company, Anheuser-Busch, was forced to respond with a statement saying, "We never intended to be part of a discussion that divides people."

I found this statement to be particularly hilarious given who was making it. You never intended to be part of a discussion that divides people? You never meant to start a fight? Aren't you . . . *alcohol*? You know? Like, hey, alcohol, if you are so concerned about not wanting people to fight, you should try . . . not being fucking alcohol? The cause of countless fights throughout human history? Like, where are we getting this idea that the alcohol you drink must Reflect Your Values? Don't people drink alcohol to *forget* their values?

Anyway, conservatives had a meltdown, many in the LGBTQ

community were upset over what it saw as the company not having Mulvaney's back regarding the controversy, and, ultimately, Anheuser-Busch saw tens of billions in market-value losses. Amid all this, a podcast interview with Bud Light's vice president of marketing, Alissa Heinerscheid, which was recorded before the controversy, started making the rounds. In the interview, Heinerscheid said she wanted to update the brand's "fratty" and "out-of-touch" (her words) branding: "I'm a businesswoman, I had a really clear job to do when I took over Bud Light, and it was 'This brand is in decline, it's been in a decline for a really long time, and if we do not attract young drinkers to come and drink this brand there will be no future for Bud Light.'"

Now, a lot has already been said about how her words made many of the brand's typical consumers angry, and I can kind of get where they're coming from . . . at least definitely more than I understood the absurdly apoplectic level of fury directed at Mulvaney over her single post with a single specially made can, even though I do find her gratingly annoying for reasons that have nothing to do with gender. For one thing, I love frat guys. My college boyfriend, aka Cheens's dad, was the president of a fraternity, making me its First Lady. Actually, as far as women in their mid-thirties go, I'm probably one of the frattier ones: *Happy Gilmore* is my favorite movie; I used to work at Barstool Sports, and not only have I drunk Bud Lights in frat houses but I've also referred to them as "crispy boys" far more often than I've used their proper name. The thing about that is, though, Heinerscheid wasn't exactly placing herself on team *Anti-Frat*, either. She wanted the brand to *appear* more inclusive, yes, but she also expressed that she wanted this specifically as "a businesswoman." It wasn't really activism, but a business decision for the sake of what a business aims to make: money. Of course, the plan turned out to be an extraordinary failure, but to me, what's far more interesting to think about than Anheuser-Busch's earnings numbers is how the whole thing impacted the rest of us: how, thanks to a single Instagram post with a single specially made can, *all* cans of Bud Light *everywhere* became politically charged, no matter who was drinking one or why—and how that really, really sucks for the people who wanted to be able to just drink their beerish water in peace. Drinking a Bud Light became open invitation for conversation about thorny sociopolitical issues, effectively removing it entirely as an option for so many.

A January 2021 paper in the *Journal of Public Policy & Marketing* examined the impacts that political polarization can have when it influences our decision-making and found that, as a piece covering the findings published on Montana State University's website put it: "[P]eople may sacrifice wages and disregard opportunities to save." It continued: "[R]esearch has found that employees accept lower wages to work for politically like-minded entities, and people may select higher-priced products or ones that offer less-functional value."

Now, it would be willfully obtuse of me to talk about all of this without noting the way that the media can contribute to politicization.

Indeed, that 2019 "perception gap" study I shared earlier in this book, regarding how *off* Democrats and Republicans were in estimating how many in the other camp held "extreme" beliefs, also found that those "who said they read the news 'most of the time' were nearly three times more distorted in their perceptions than those who said they read the news 'only now and then.'"

A lot of what I have to say about "Fox News" as a lightning rod, I've already said in other chapters, but I'll add this, too: The people on the Left who treat the existence of a Right-leaning outlet as a uniquely and unconscionably awful abomination conveniently ignore how it came to be in the first place, which was as an antidote to the media's heretofore largely liberal slant. It's also hypocritical and narrow-minded to act as if the Left doesn't have many partisan-leaning outlets of its own. It does! In fact, a study from Syracuse University's Newhouse School of Public Communications found that just 3.4 percent of American journalists are Republicans.

Now, I want to make it clear that I'm not calling for anything to be done about any of this. Or, more accurately, it's that nothing *can* be done about it, which is a major reason why I'm not compelled to spend too much more time talking about it.

Given that whole First Amendment thing, after all, a media entity is free to lean whichever way it wants, which is certainly better than the alternative! Giving government the power to enact limits would be forfeiting a crucial check that we have on their overall control.

Plus, the partisan-news-outlet genie really is just totally out of the bottle. So the only way to deal with any anger or hurt or pain over the current media landscape is something I learned in therapy called "radical acceptance." (Yeah . . . in case you couldn't tell earlier when I asked you if something "fit with the facts," I have been to a lot of therapy.) Anyway, "radical acceptance" is the complete and total (you guessed it!) acceptance of things as they are. By truly letting go of any illusion of control, you're also releasing any bitterness or temptation to throw any tantrums about how unfair it is, because, well, there's nothing you can do about it anyway, so why bother wasting your energy and time?

I mean, what *would* you do about it, even if you could? Force people to switch the channels they watch? I'm not sure that would work anyway: Remember that research I shared that found altering algorithms and feeds on social media not only didn't help decrease polarization but also worsened it in some cases? I see no reason why the results wouldn't be similar regarding other mediums, too.

Now, radical acceptance of the fact that there's nothing anyone can do to stop the existence of partisan-leaning media doesn't mean there's nothing we can do to combat polarization overall. Like in the case of Big Tech, placing the blame on some powerful, untouchable conglomerate is a cop-out, because it allows you to place all the responsibility there, too—when really, it is up to us to question what we see and hear and to be curiously open to listening, learning, and kindness, no matter how futile it can seem at times to try.

In the same breath, I've never said you should blindly trust and agree with everything you hear on Fox News or anywhere else. You should always think critically!

The possible pitfalls of Media as a Business came up when Danica Patrick interviewed me for her *Pretty Intense* podcast, asking, "Where do you see a pathway for people in the news to be able to just be honest, it doesn't have to follow a color [referring to the Red or Blue partisan teams] or a belief system based on the channel you're on, can we get there?"

For one thing, I explained to her, I *personally* was *already* there.

I added, though, that I also think the temptation to fall in line has become far greater because of what I led this chapter discussing: all the hate you'll have to actually *see* because of social media. People who use social media to eviscerate strangers is a small—and obviously the least well-adjusted—segment of the population, but it can sometimes feel overwhelming in the moment. This is even though I've spent so much time asking myself, my friends, and my audience the same question about the hateful commenters, which is: *Who are these people?* I have been watching TV for a lot longer than I've been on it, and I've certainly come across personalities whom I don't like. What I haven't done, though, is taken that extra step to be like, *Better let her know!* Better log on and reach out to her to tell her that she's a slut, that her voice and her laugh and her face are annoying, that her forehead's too big, that she's too skinny, that her eggs are drying up and she had better get pregnant, but actually, don't get pregnant *ever*, because you're a selfish miserable bitch who only cares about herself and you'd make a terrible mother, and she's seriously so stupid, whose dick did she suck to get where she is, replace her with XYZ, I fast-forward through her parts because she makes me sick, you can tell Greg hates her, I'm a total stranger who has never met either one of them but I *know* that Greg hates her and he would want me to be on here calling her a dumb talentless whore, she doesn't deserve her spot on the show, she doesn't deserve anything, she's worthless, she's secretly a communist, she's secretly a man . . . *Who are these people*, who feel the need to tell me these things? Like, just talk shit about me from your couch or in your group chat like a normal, decent person. I've ranted about this everywhere, from my live shows to *Gutfeld!* (The latter of which I ended by shouting, "Hot girls have big foreheads!")

Again, I've never let any of it keep me from being forthright. Or, as I told Danica: "We really are in a tough spot where people are so afraid to speak . . . everything is so polarized . . . I feel like, if I have this platform, I just owe it to . . . I'm not religious, so I don't know what I owe it to, but I wouldn't feel right about" not doing it that way.

Danica suggested to me that she actually might know why I was doing it: "I'm going to bet it's because it's changed your life . . . we tend to advocate for anything we're super sold on . . . like man, I tried that low-carb diet, it really worked, and you just want to tell everyone."

I think she was right! Overall, many viewers have, over time, come to trust me more due to the exact same reason that I've been yelled at by some of them sometimes. Dozens of the people I met during my first tour told me that they have come to trust the fact that, whether they agree or disagree with something that I've said, they're at least confident that I must be saying it only because I do believe it.

Honestly, I feel hope whenever people tell me they share my concerns about how divided we're becoming as the demands for partisan purity become stricter. What's more, it reminds me of how the effectiveness of politicizing certain issues can make our discussions about them ineffective.

Partisanship and politicization can convince people to dismiss an entire human being over something as small as a joke about a country singer. The more things that we turn into politically partisan

Left/Right litmus tests—like beer and country music artists—the more specific list of likes and dislikes a person will need to (at least pretend to) adhere to in order to avoid being seen as irredeemable by a huge swath of the population, and the harder it will be for us to see value in one other. If we don't stay vigilant about the litmus test list as it's growing, we'll wind up with more issues going the way of climate change—that is, issues that become unquestionably partisan, likely *exactly because* we've stopped bothering to question them. Again: Thinking about it, how has caring about the planet come to equal an entire political identity as a Leftist? How has caring about the consequences of imposing certain costs become a marker of the Right? It seems inexplicable, and that's probably because we rarely, if ever, even bother to explain it, perhaps even to ourselves. We need to keep checking in with ourselves about the possible motivations, financial or otherwise, and questioning whether the issue or comment we've accepted as a partisan litmus test for an entire political identity is not only accurate but also worth everything we might lose.

5

Half-Veteran

On my very first date with Cam, he told me he was a West Point grad who fought in Afghanistan circa 2012–13. I told him he had fought in a good-for-nothing war.

If you think that was a stupid, cruel thing for me to say to a hero? That I must have really pissed him off, because everybody knows that the only proper response to someone's announcement of past military service is to thank them for it, much like saying "God bless you!" to a sneeze or "Congratulations!" to the news that a person is pregnant, even though it's with a baby that literally no one has even met yet? If you can't believe that he found it within his valiant heart to marry a rude, dismissive, unpatriotic brat like me, even after I had shown myself to be so offensive, willingly setting himself up for a life of social-concepts anarchy? I'll crush those biases in just a few pages, because only that last phrase is true.

First, I want to acknowledge that my relationship with Cam is in itself a triumph over biases—my own. I remember not liking him at all. The first time I laid eyes on him, I immediately started racking my brain for what might be a believable excuse to leave our date in an hour or less.

Why didn't I like him? Well, first, he was a hedge fund guy . . . and he dressed like one. I'm talking full-on Finance Douche uniform. I'd never dated a finance guy before in my life, for no other reason except for I just didn't find them attractive. He had a suit jacket on, and the shirt underneath was tucked in. His hair was done, which meant that this man not only owned hair products but also used them. I don't think I even need to tell you this part, but yes, he was wearing loafers.

Anyway, all the excuses I tried just weren't working, so there was only one thing to do: drink five tequila sodas. It was a bit more fun after that, because, well, what *isn't* fun after five tequila sodas? Plus, he was so addicted to the Juul that he couldn't help hitting it inside of the bar, and I was the same way at the time. He even convinced me to go to a second location, where I ended up kissing him before leaving.

In case you are confused and/or Mormon: I did not end up kissing him because he'd worked his way into my skeptical heart by the end of the date, putting us on the path to love. I ended up kissing him because I'd had five tequila sodas. Keep up.

While I wasn't really feeling him, Cam felt the opposite: He was super into me right off the bat. Not to brag; that's just the truth. And even though he had managed to surprise me in some ways, I was still just kind of afraid he might be too conservative or judgmental or basic. He didn't have any tattoos. He had a good job. He came from a good family. He went to boarding school. He seemed sane and well-adjusted, like he might calmly discuss our way through a disagreement without calling me any names, blocking me on Instagram, or disappearing on me for weeks—and I'd really become accustomed to the kind of, you know, *pizzazz* that an untreated mental illness can bring to a relationship.

I get that a healthy, conventionally attractive man in his right mind sounds like what people are looking for, but it's certainly not what I was into. Just take a look at the kinds of people I'd been seeing before him: an abusive narcissist (hereinafter referred to as Nightmare of a Boyfriend); more than one person with substance abuse issues; a neck-tatted Cuban dad who told me not to have kids because "your body is never the same" (I hadn't asked him his opinion); another neck-tatted single dad; a wannabe actor who cried constantly . . . you get the picture.

There was also the comedy writer. We'd been seeing each other casually in the dating sense, but actually really cared about and loved each other as friends on top of that, usually texting back and forth throughout most days. I was at the gyno for my Pap smear staring at my phone and wondering why he hadn't texted me back when I instead received the news that he'd been found dead—forcing me to same-day cancel my second date with Cam for the second time because I was so devastated. (Man, the people in the waiting room who watched me sob and choke and struggle to pay my bill must have thought I'd just found out that there was something *really* wrong with my vagina.)

Anyway, I finally did decide to go on the third-scheduled second date with Cam after a lot of prodding from my sister, as well as my friend Elisha, both of whom asked me: "Well, sure, he's not your type, but Kat . . . how *has* your type been working for you?" They may have just been watching too much *Dr. Phil*, but damn, those bitches were right.

For that third-scheduled second date, Cam picked a restaurant located just steps away from his apartment. For the second-scheduled second date, he would later tell me, he had pulled out all the stops: a fancy, hard-to-get-into restaurant, everything. But for the three-times-you're-out second date, not so much: He showed up late, unshaven and wearing a hat. And I remember thinking as soon as he walked in—damn, he's *hot*. We never spent a night apart after that and moved in together four months later.

I was happy, which, for me, was terrifying—and not just because everyone in my life from Greg Gutfeld to Dr. Drew to my own father kept telling me: *"Do not fuck this up."* It was also because, if I'm being honest with myself, I'm pretty sure that part of the reason I went for mentally unstable losers was not only because of the spark, but also because I felt there was less of a risk of me absolutely hating myself if I did fuck it up with those guys. If those guys walked out on me, or, more accurately, *when* those guys *did* walk out on me, I could always tell myself: "Whatever, who cares, that guy's a loser anyway" . . . until they came back. (And they always did come back.) I guess it didn't matter much to my subconscious that this meant-to-be-consolation didn't ever even work for me. Instead of telling myself: "Whatever, who cares, that guy's a loser anyway," what I would tell myself wound up being more along the lines of: *"I am so awful that not even a total loser like Cries So Much I Don't Know How He Can Even Manage to Wait Tables wants me!"* Completely ignoring, apparently, that a root cause of my issues with those men was that I knew deep down, and in conversations with my friends, that I could never truly, fully commit to the likes of them.

Of course, there was another concern about surrendering myself (gag, I know) to a traditional healthy relationship and—trigger warning, if you're eating, stop reading because it's pretty gross—I was worried what a happy relationship would do *to my brand.*

This, on top of the general concerns that many Career-Driven Women have about a man getting in the way of reaching their goals, was a specific concern because of my specific path. By this point, I'd made a name for myself by laughing at my loneliness. If you read my first book, *You Can't Joke About That,* you'll know that I was dumped in front of my dad at Coney Island just days before getting hired at Fox News. If you've seen me on *Gutfeld!,* you've probably heard at least five stories about my past failed relationships.

I will never forget my first Valentine's Day after Cam and I started seeing each other—I'm talking still-receiving-texts-from-my-former-roster new—just a week or two after that second date. I hadn't told anyone other than my close friends about him yet, and, although I was into him, I didn't even really know how to do any of this. Instead,

I did what I did know how to do, and had already been doing that week: fire off a bunch of my signature snarky tweets about Valentine's Day, such as:

It is hard for me to focus on Feb 13th bc I am too excited to see pics of all of your flowers tmw. Plz do not forget to post them on all platforms, & whatever you do, do NOT forget to let me know whether or not the person who gave them to you is the best boyfriend IN THE WORLD

When posting pictures of your flowers today, please don't forget to also let me know whether or not your boyfriend is *also* your best friend and partner in crime.

Remember that you can buy your own damn self flowers and also to watch me on #Kennedy tonight!

But my cover was about to be blown. Cam's mom, who apparently had been watching my tweets for years, told Cam he should buy me flowers. He did, and they were delivered during a recording of the *Tyrus and Timpf* podcast.

I'll never forget it. At the very start of the podcast, I got a phone call and had to go downstairs to get a delivery.

When I returned with the roses, Tyrus mocked me for being happy, and said the fact that I was happy meant I was not going to be funny anymore.

Throughout the episode, I insisted that I had not lost my gray cloud and denied that I was happy, even though you could clearly hear in my voice that I was smiling.

But as much as I tried to minimize it, my transformation was big news. So much so that, during another episode of our show, special guest Dr. Drew mentioned within minutes that all he wanted to talk about was "how Kat has changed."

The two of them went back and forth about my past relationships, mainly that abusive one—which Drew compared to an intravenous heroin addiction, mind you—and interrogated me about how I might possibly perform my stand-up set that night when I'd lost all my dark material.

"My set's going to be like a time capsule of my life," I said, still completely unable to even fathom the possibility that I could ever draw material from anything but darkness and disarray.

None of this was a bit. As happy as I was to be falling in love—not just love, but *requited*, healthy love—I was also completely freaked out that this happy love story would mean that my career was completely over.

This kind of love was honestly not something that I ever earnestly searched for. Actually, my disinterest in it had started at a very young age: When I would watch Disney movies as a toddler, and the princess would get her man, I couldn't even comprehend how that alone might be a happy ending. Instead, I would turn and ask my parents: "Okay, but what does *she* want to do?" I was far too young to understand a single thing about love, but seeing a fantasy love story left me mostly with concerns about what it might mean for the princess's career. Similarly, I remember once asking an aunt why all the songs on the radio were always about love when there was so much other stuff in life.

These concerns only grew as I did: Thirty-year-old me wasn't only afraid how of a relationship might distract me from my career goals, but also of how it would dry up the well of dating-disasters material that I'd been relying on for so many years.

My biases told me that I couldn't have a healthy relationship and a flourishing career; they told me that I couldn't be happy and funny. But the opposite turned out to be true: My career skyrocketed so rapidly after I'd started dating Cam that there's no way it could have been a coincidence. Not only did the relationship turn out to not be a distraction, but it also turned out that I'd been far more distracted before it. No longer having to worry about whatever issue I was having with whatever loser freed up a lot of space in my brain.

What I feared would make me unfunny was also wrong. Sure, the old well of material had dried up—but now, I had a new one. For instance, I have a recurring joke on the show that I am, by virtue of being married to a West Point–trained Army Ranger, a Half-Veteran. "Once you get married, everything gets split in half, therefore, I am half of a veteran."

For the haters: I don't believe that is literally true; not only is it a joke, but also, I am the punchline of it. Cam went to Afghanistan; I didn't; I can't take half of that. I can't imagine what it was like to shoot and be shot at. Of course I can't! In my case, the absurdity of the label is the joke's entire point.

That's not to say that some military spouses don't at least come close to earning that label, if not definitely earning it, considering the burdens that they bear regarding their spouses' service. They do. By the time I started dating Cam, he was long out of the service, so I don't really count myself among them. I can't compare myself, for example, to a woman raising kids alone because their dad was killed in combat. That's not to say I've never had to see Cam struggle, or that I haven't learned more about the military—including the sacrifices it takes to get there and the way that putting yourself into a combat environment can impact the rest of your life—from my marriage, because I have.

For example: In the summer of 2021, President Biden was set on having all United States troops out of Afghanistan by Sept. 11, 2021, in honor of the twenty-year anniversary of the 9/11 attacks.

On July 8, Biden promised that a Taliban-controlled Afghanistan was "highly unlikely." And yet that is exactly what happened a mere five weeks later.

The fall of Afghanistan to the Taliban was a difficult time for Cam, who had lost classmates in combat. Knowing I had no understanding whatsoever of what he was going through, and knowing just as well that, despite that, *I* would be the one discussing the issue in front of millions of people on television, I asked him as many questions as I could.

Cam explained to me that when he had been there for a combat mission about eight years earlier, he *knew then* that what the United States declared as its goal, to set up a Westernized army for the Afghan government that would prevent the country from becoming a sanctuary for terrorists, was not feasible. For one thing, he told me, setting up a Westernized army for the Afghan government would require teaching people who didn't even know how to read how to use equipment that was, as he put it, "highly sophisticated" and "required a baseline level of education" across several different disciplines.

Of course, I'd had a similar take on that first date of ours, in which I called Afghanistan a useless war, and I hadn't been there myself. (I hadn't seen any good all-inclusive packages.) And although my own knowledge could never compare to firsthand knowledge from someone like Cam, it's also not like I'd just spouted that stuff out on a first date for no reason, or even that the reason was just tequila. I'd based my opinion on, for example, what those of us paying attention learned after the release of the Afghanistan Papers in 2019, which found that top military guys were even going so far as to manipulate statistics to paint a rosier picture to politicians of how things were going.

Or, as Bob Crowley, an Army colonel and a senior counterinsurgency adviser to commanders in 2013 and 2014, put it in an interview with the Office of the Special Inspector General for Afghan Reconstruction: "Every data point was altered to present the best picture possible. Surveys, for instance, were totally unreliable but reinforced that everything we were doing was right and we became a self-licking ice cream cone."

"We spent a trillion dollars there equipping people and training Afghan soldiers. And twenty years later this all falls apart within a month?" I asked on *The Five* at the time.

Or, as I said on *Gutfeld!* that week, in part:

All these guys at the top, they knew, and they still kept coming out, and giving these rosy pronouncements of what was going on over there, and they're getting promoted, they're sitting on the boards of companies—my husband's been very upset saying, "Hey, I agreed that I would have given my life for this country."

And all of these people at the top cared more about their power and the money in their pockets than they cared about his life . . . [H]e went to West Point; lost four classmates in Afghanistan alone. There needs to be an investigation . . . I mean a trillion dollars equipping and training these people and it all falls apart so quickly like this?

If this were anything else? There would have been investigation, accountability, but because the military-industrial complex props everything up, they're getting away with it. We're talking about a huge amount of money, talking about human lives, and there's no actual responsibilities. It's disgusting.

Fire takes, amiright? Credit goes to Cam.

The administration seemed to move on quickly—so quickly, in fact, that I remember feeling a level of gaslighted that I'd historically only felt from someone I was fucking, with me tweeting on August 18: **Biden showing up to give a whole speech about booster shots without even mentioning Afghanistan reminds me of the time a guy I was seeing screamed at me and called me horrible names and then just texted me "Hey how are you babe" a few days later like nothing happened.**

But Cam hadn't moved on. He kept telling me that it was going to get much worse. At his birthday brunch a few days later, he shared with the table what he'd been sharing with me: Closing the Bagram Air Base was a mistake; there was going to be a major, deadly attack at the airport in Kabul. The American soldiers were standing too close together; they didn't know what they were doing. This wasn't their fault; it's just that they were trained for nation-building, not for combat, and it was infuriating that the leaders tossed these kids into this risky situation to get out of Afghanistan on a symbolic date for a symbolic victory. Young people were going to lose their lives for a perceived opportunity for political points, and shame on senior leadership for putting them in this position.

And that is, of course, exactly what happened: Before August was over, a suicide bomber would attack the Kabul airport, killing thirteen U.S. servicemembers—eleven of whom *were* very young, between the ages of twenty and twenty-three.

When the U.S. State Department finally released its report on the withdrawal in July 2023, it placed the blame a lot of the same places that Cam had—failures of senior leadership, the closing of the Bagram Air Base, and the need to rush to meet Biden's symbolic deadline. It also admitted that there had been a lack of experienced people involved, but also dared to try to pin that on pandemic-related staffing challenges. Weak!

Basically, the report made the admission that a lot could have been done differently, but not without heaps of excuses for why it wasn't. What's more, it stopped far short of calling for anything that comes even remotely close to a consequence for anyone who messed it up. Hell, it even went so far as to praise them.

In other words? The United States military is either unable or unwilling to do what I did at the age of thirty when I finally agreed to go on that second date with Cam: realize that what I had been doing in the past wasn't working, that I could only explain that away for so long before I'd just be cheating myself out of a better future, that the types of guys I kept trusting weren't producing the kinds of results that I wanted, and it was time to confront that reality, stop doing what I had been doing, and to start doing something (someone?) new.

The need to do something differently is obvious to anyone paying attention, but the government bypasses this by instead doing what I'm trying so hard to bring attention to in this book: turning us against each other with politics and manipulative narratives.

Often, the narratives are rooted in partisanship. Remember when President Barack Obama was awarded the Nobel Prize for Peace in 2009, less than eight months into his presidency? It seemed at first premature, and then eventually like a total joke to anyone unbiased, considering that the ceremony wound up taking place just days after Obama declared that he would be sending 30,000 more troops into Afghanistan.

In September 2013, when I was in Los Angeles as part of my work for a writing fellowship, I went to the University of California to ask students about whether they felt that then-President Obama deserved the award.

Answering that question was easy: Yes!

What was more difficult, apparently, was my follow-up question: Why?

"I just feel like in general being a good guy, it's just creating a lot more peace and like, mellow," said one student, adding, "I love Obama, and I love everything he is doing. I just feel like everyone is so hard on him and it's only his second year."

When I asked one student what the difference was between President Obama and President Bush invading the Middle East, she replied: "Bush, I just didn't like him. I just don't."

If you want to see the video of these interviews, I'm pretty sure it's still online. If not, suffice it to say that a lot of the answers for why Obama deserved the Nobel Peace Prize had nothing to do with the prize or his policies; it was just that they liked Obama. It wasn't about deeds; it was about partisanship. To these students and so many other people, Obama was on The Good Side, so the things he did were Good Things.

Of course, when it comes to military issues, the manipulative narratives aren't always drawn along partisan lines. Unfortunately, I don't mean this in a good way—I mean that, too often, agreeing to feed us bullshit regarding war is one of the few things that we've seen the two parties be able to unite around.

Repeatedly, we've seen those who have dared to question military intervention be smeared and written off because of it.

For example: Three days after 9/11, California Democratic Rep. Barbara Lee was the only member of Congress who voted against giving the government the broad military authorization it would use for the war in Afghanistan, explaining: "[W]e must be careful not to embark on an open-ended war with neither an exit strategy nor a focused target," and pleading, "[w]e cannot repeat past mistakes."

Her concern was completely legitimate—and, as time would reveal, very well-founded.

At the time, though, she suffered greatly for this vote: death threats, the need for full-time security, and, of course, countless accusations of traitorousness.

A few years later, we'd see intolerance for questioning the war in Iraq, to the point that it was extremely rare to hear it at all: In the two weeks prior to the invasion, ABC, CBS, NBC, and PBS would have only one out of their 267 American guests question it, according to Fairness and Accuracy in Reporting. According to a review of Pew Research Center surveys, public support for the war "was built, at least in part, on a foundation of falsehoods," such as the belief that Saddam Hussein had weapons of mass destruction.

It's been a consistent pattern. Or, as Pulitzer Prize–winning journalist Chris Hedges put it in a column in July 2023:

> The playbook the pimps of war use to lure us into one military
> fiasco after another, including Vietnam, Afghanistan, Iraq, Libya,
> Syria and now Ukraine, does not change. Freedom and democracy
> are threatened. Evil must be vanquished. Human rights must be

protected. The fate of Europe and NATO, along with a "rules-based international order" is at stake. Victory is assured.

The results are also the same. The justifications and narratives are exposed as lies. The cheery prognosis is false.

More recently, questioning or exploring alternatives to the United States' involvement in Russia's war on Ukraine has been enough to get you labeled a Putin Puppet. In October 2022, a group of thirty House Democrats sent a letter to President Biden asking him to consider using diplomacy to end it—certainly a reasonable suggestion, considering that the conflict was supposed to last only a few days and was now raging eighteen months later, especially when the government you're petitioning has such a long, consistent track record of having lied to the public about the realities of its military involvements in the past. Despite this, though, the backlash to the letter was so bad (Democratic Sen. Chris Murphy, for example, declared that "Vladimir Putin would have signed that letter if asked") that the signatories withdrew it less than twenty-four hours later, explaining that it had been "released by staff without vetting."

Of course, there has already been some evidence that our government has been lying to us about this war, too. In April 2023, a document leak revealed that the Biden administration had been misleading the public about how well Ukraine was faring in the conflict. Media outlets including NPR, Vice News, and the *Washington Post* focused on how wrong the leaker was for leaking, rather than how wrong the government was for lying to us and taking our money to fund something it had been leading us to believe was going far better than it really was—with *WaPo*'s editorial criticizing only his betrayal by revealing the secrets, and not even *mentioning* the government betrayal that it had revealed.

It's not like there's no reason for the United States to want the war to continue. For one thing, like all wars, it makes weapons manufacturers rich—and "weapons manufacturer" is what military officials can pretty much expect they'll end up doing after their time in the military ends. In fact, a Quincy Institute for Responsible Statecraft report released in October 2023 found that more than 80 percent of "four-star officers who retired after June 2018 . . . went to work for the arms industry as board members, advisors, executives, consultants, lobbyists, or members of financial institutions that invest in the defense sector." They don't call it "military-industrial complex" for nothing, bro!

Now, I am sure some would write off my concerns as those of an alt-Right Putin sympathizer—which is, I guess, easier than realizing that I had the same take when it came to Edward Snowden and Julian Assange as I did regarding the Ukraine-secrets leaker. But the politicization of questioning the Ukraine war has, to an extent, run along partisan lines—just the opposite ones that they were before. In this case, questioning a war makes you far-Right.

But the fact that so many people would have made this rush to judgment illustrates the problem: Black-and-white binary thinking—whether it's along partisan lines, or more of a cross-partisan pressure to write off an entire person as traitorous for simply asking a question about a war—has been fueling the military-industrial complex for decades. No matter how many times those making the warnings have turned out to be right, it still seems like a lesson we simply cannot learn. This is even though it hurts every single one of us, minus those who gain wealth through it, like those weapons companies, or power through wartime measures that are purportedly for our safety, like the Patriot Act. In general, whenever I hear language from the government that's clearly meant to evoke fear, I ask myself two questions: Who or what does the government want me to be afraid of? And what do they gain if they succeed?

Honestly? To me, it seems clear that, the more pressure you feel to *not* question something, the more important it is *to* question it. Whether it's regarding that abusive Nightmare of a Boyfriend storming out of my apartment and ghosting me for weeks if I dared to ask him why this girl was texting him at three in the morning (only to find her name on a list of seventeen people he had slept with that year in a notebook he left in my apartment sometime later) or a warmonger smearing you as a traitor for questioning the war machine (only to find out that what had been paraded around as patriotism was actually propaganda), there is often no clearer sign that someone seeks to hide reality by forbidding you from even thinking about questioning it in order to maintain control.

With everything so polarized, and the prevailing objective too often being to dunk on the Other Side—The Bad Side!—at the expense of examining your own, it is so easy for the government to simply do whatever it wants to do unchecked.

It's become increasingly clear that talking points about war tend to be nothing more than that. It was just a few short years ago, after all, that my noninterventionist views were a point of agreement that liberals had with me, and a reason for conservatives to attack me. As soon as former President Trump started singing a different tune on this issue, however, the sides flipped. Then, many conservatives started to agree with what I've been saying, while liberals were quick to reduce the views I've always had to nothing more than unprincipled, pro-Russia sentiments to support My Boy Trump, a guy whom I've never even voted for.

The truth would be too obvious to need to be said if the need for it to be said weren't so obvious: There are very, very few Americans who are actually sympathetic to, let alone *agents of*, hostile foreign governments. In fact, so many of the people who regret past wars or question current ones are veterans themselves. It's not just my husband. A Pew Research study published in July 2019 found that just 33 percent of veterans said that the Iraq War was worth it, with 64 percent saying that it wasn't. That's even higher than the general public's views on the issue, which were 32 and 62 percent, respectively.

The best way to fight the system is to stop allowing it to make us so readily fight one another.

When you write someone off based on differences, you could really be missing out on a better life. I would have missed out on an entire marriage if I had let my preconceived notions about Westchester prep schoolboys get in the way, or been too intimidated by the differences to realize what a great team the two of us made. (And there have been many, many differences. I'll never forget going to his family's house for Easter to meet them for the first time. They were eating *ribs* with *forks and knives*. I had no idea how to navigate that, so I just ate a plate of mostly mashed potatoes and peas. I mean, in my family, we eat ham with our hands!)

But there doesn't have to be a marriage on the other side of a misconception to make questioning it worth it. It could be something else! When it comes to war, it could be something as simple as, you know, avoiding needless loss of money and human lives and the forfeiture of the rights that even more lives have been lost fighting for us to have.

6

Mental Health Issues Can Drive You Crazy

In August 2023, this headline from the *New York Post* popped up on my phone: "Robert O'Neill, former Navy SEAL who killed Osama bin Laden, arrested in Texas."

And then, moments later: "Former Navy SEAL Robert O'Neill, who killed Bin Laden, called security guard N-word during arrest: sources."

Full disclosure, Rob and his wife are good friends of me and my husband. Specifics aside, my reaction was one that most humans could understand, but most internet mobs would deem inexcusable: I was worried about my friends.

Oh, you should also know that not only did Rob deny using the language the second headline claimed he had, but, days later, *The Post* published another headline, reading: "Security guard who claimed ex-Navy SEAL Robert O'Neill called him N-word revealed to be a white man."

In any case! Regardless of whether or not the dude was white, and even regardless of whether or not Rob really did use the slur, his behavior was still not okay—passing out at the hotel bar and then hitting a security guard who is just trying to help you to your room is absolutely not okay. Unacceptable. But there's already been endless discussion about how Not Okay it all was, and, so, I'd rather have the conversation that no one was having—one that I have until now been too afraid to start, except for in a flurry of text messages to my husband that week:

> I am so upset about Rob O'Neill. What's more fucked up: What he did, or what the government does to our men in making them fight to enrich themselves?
> I could cry.
> Absolutely fucked up what he did. That's easy to say. What's harder to acknowledge is that a government-trained killer might have a tough time adjusting to normal life, to resort to substance, and more so after seeing that what he fought for was bullshit.

Anyway, here I won't get into the bullshit that the government feeds us regarding war; that's what my "Half-Veteran" chapter was about.

Here, I want to get into something else, which is a brand of bullshit that belongs to civilians, too: spouting "Support the Troops!" without thinking about what that even means.

Of course, in this instance, I had the benefit of actually knowing Rob, so I didn't need to work to see him as a human. My husband and I had already heard about some of his struggles—things that, no, I absolutely will not share here because I am not a backstabbing blabbermouth press-and-cash-hungry dickhead. (Looking at you, Prince Harry.)

What I will share is what Rob himself shared on his podcast after the incident:

> Think about your darkest secret. Think about something you do that's shameful, that no one really knows about, that you don't brag about. Stuff you do when the doors are locked . . . you know what I'm talking about, we're all there with something. My dark secret just happened to get blasted all over the world

and that's something that I don't wish upon anybody . . . people on the internet don't care about your feelings . . . other people like to glorify themselves based on your failures . . . But mine got blasted all over the world; you know what mine is now. Sometimes, and this has been an issue, I try to numb some of the pain with drinking vodka. And it's not like the fun times going out when you're young . . . this is just more of a "I want to just drink to get rid of the pain" . . . kind of like the opening scene in *Leaving Las Vegas* when Nic Cage has the shopping cart in the store . . . He's trying to drink himself to death . . . I've been doing this for a while, and it is one of those things where the only way you can fix yourself is by admitting it at first to yourself . . . The process of trying to fix yourself is the realization that you can ask for help and it's okay . . . What happened in Texas, some positives have come out of it. I've had a lot of Navy SEALs reach out to me, a lot of veterans reach out to me, and it's sort of one of those things almost where we don't really talk about it, but a lot of people have the same problems.

He goes on to say that he planned to try new avenues for seeking help with his issues with alcohol, adding: "Once you hit rock bottom, there's only one way to go, and that's back up."

According to the U.S. Department of Veterans Affairs, roughly 1 in 10 veterans returning from the wars in Iraq and Afghanistan who are seen at a VA clinic have a drug or alcohol problem. Nearly 1 out of 3 of those seeking treatment for Substance Use Disorder (SUD) have PTSD, and of those with PTSD, more than 2 out of 10 also have SUD. So, yeah, it indeed is, as Rob put it, "a lot."

Thinking of the phrase "Support the Troops!" probably paints a patriotic, pretty picture in your mind. Wearing a lapel pin on your suit. Commemorating Memorial Day on your Instagram page. Smiling at an old man wearing a "veteran" hat on an airplane and telling him, "Thank you for your service."

The reality, though, is that supporting people who have fought for this country can be far too ugly for Instagram. Dealing with an individual who struggles with substance abuse, for example, can be anything but pretty. It's brutal. It's frustrating, scary, infuriating, and often all-consuming. It can demand a level of patience and grace that exhausts you physically, emotionally, and spiritually, and through it all you're still faced with the hopeless, harsh reality that you don't even know if anything you do will end up doing any good anyway.

There was nothing Instagrammable about Rob's behavior. It was out of line, and his past military service certainly does not give him license to behave however he wants.

But the thing is, you can totally acknowledge that while also asking yourself: If *I* spent more than a decade and a half of *my* life as a government-trained killer—shooting and being shot at—am I confident that I would handle what comes with that any better? Am I sure I wouldn't have any sort of drunken meltdown of my own? It's easy to put your hand over your heart when the national anthem comes on; it's much harder to see a person's humanity when it's trapped beneath a public pile-on.

This sort of exercise can be useful even when the person in question isn't a veteran. There are, after all, many mental health–related refrains that get repeated and reposted. For example: Whenever a celebrity dies by suicide, you'll see a lot of the same posts on the Instagram pages of everyone else. Things like: "You are not alone. If you are feeling depressed or suicidal, please call hotline XYZ," and "If you feel like you're not worth it, I promise you that you are. I love you, and I'm here for you. Share if you agree."

It's not that spreading awareness is a bad thing. It's good! But posts like those ignore some tough truths. A hotline post ignores that people with depression are, by the very nature of their illness, a lot less likely to actually make that kind of call. Feeling hopeless means that you don't see any hope, and feeling worthless means you might not feel like you deserve saving. Shouting "YOU'RE WORTH IT, I LOVE YOU, I'M HERE" ignores the fact that, well, people in the depths of depression or mental illness are sometimes the most difficult, exhausting people to have in your life. When I think back to my own darkest times, I feel not only grateful but also absolutely terrible for everyone who somehow managed to stick by my side. Like substance abuse, it's anything but pretty, no matter what colors an organization uses for its aesthetically pleasing awareness graphics.

Now, it's true that we've never talked more openly about the importance of mental health than we have in recent years. Despite this, in December 2022, "Americans' positive self-assessments of their mental health" were "the lowest in more than two decades of Gallup polling."

There are likely lots of reasons for this, but I'm not the only one who notices the juxtaposition. In a September 2023 interview with psychologist Lucy Foulkes, *NewScientist* asked, "It feels like there is a mental health awareness campaign almost every week. Surely that is a good thing?"

Foulkes replied:

> It seems like it is, but I think there are all sorts of reasons why it might not be. These campaigns are often designed for social media, posters, billboards or whatever, so they are necessarily very shallow when, actually, mental health is an incredibly complex topic. They tell people to go and get help, and the help often isn't there. A lot of campaigns are encouraging people to talk and not enough are teaching people to listen.

To me, a major reason for the juxtaposition might be the difference between the way we talk about mental health and tolerance and understanding and the way we actually handle these issues when we're confronted with them. Our culture has never talked more openly about the importance of mental health, sure, but we also seem to live in a time that gives the absolute least leeway to the people we see publicly going through mental health issues. Often, strangers online will see someone who's going through something and assign the least charitable interpretation to their behavior. Not only in their minds but also publicly, and sometimes even tagging them in it. It's happened to me!

I've never been to war, but I have been on Accutane. And yeah, I know that's nowhere near the same thing, and I also know that the amount of anxiety I get just being around a game of Jenga is enough to prove there's no way I could handle going, either.

The data on Accutane and depression is reportedly "mixed," but, being on it made me feel like I wanted to die. I felt like I was good-for-nothing and there was nothing I could even do to ever feel any better. I've managed depression, anxiety, and ADHD since I can remember, but even so, My Accutane Journey was a level of absolute despondence I've never felt before or since, a difference that was noticed clearly not just by me, but by the people in my life as well.

The rock-bottom moment when I decided to stop taking it for good was when Cam found me lying on my bathroom floor—which is gross enough, as I share it with Cheens and his litter box; it's The Timpf Bathroom—and crying because, as I put it to him then, *"Everyone I know is going to die, and I'm gonna die too!"*

Of course, that was all true and had always been, but before Accutane, it had been true without leaving me sobbing on the bathroom floor on a random weeknight because of it. (Stone-cold sober, I might add. For those of you who don't know, you can't drink on the drug.)

This was the final-straw meltdown, but it wasn't the first. There was one that happened on Friday, June 9, and I know that because I felt incapable of making it all the way home afterward, opting to cry and write about my feelings alone in my office instead. (Well, that and texting people about my feelings with a level of raw, emotional ferality that probably made the people I was texting want to fling their phones into the river just to make it fucking stop. I meant it when I said it earlier, but I will say it again: So many of you who post "If you're struggling, I'm here to talk!" might not realize that a person in a mental health crisis is probably the last person you will actually want to talk to.)

Since we're all friends here, I'll share some of my journal with you:

I am writing this from my office on Friday, June 9 at 9:25 pm. I have been crying for two hours, my makeup smeared all over my face, a single glue-on eyelash still clinging for its sexy life on my lid, and dressed in a tight leather dress that I wore to look hot.

Honestly? If I didn't know myself and I saw me, I'd probably guess that the girl I was looking at was a streetwalking hooker, down bad on her luck even more than normal. Like, maybe she'd just discovered that the methamphetamine she'd purchased with her earnings from a long, exhausting day of sucking dick was actually just baby powder, and she knew that the only thing she could do now was find even more dick to suck and try to buy some again.

Actually, there's really just one difference between how I'd see her and how I currently see myself: I wouldn't judge her as being worthless, or her situation as being hopeless. (Plus, what bullshit that she couldn't report her fraudulent business transaction to the authorities because the laws somehow write her off as a criminal and not a victim!)

My situation, on the other hand? I do see it as hopeless.

And what is the situation, you might ask, that I feel so powerless over? The one I am treating as far more insurmountable than a late-stage methamphetamine addiction?

The teleprompter.

Yeah, bro. The fucking teleprompter. The thing that any random

former athlete with a career's worth of head injuries can figure out,
I somehow cannot manage.

Now, to be fair, I did have some issues with a mental block regarding the teleprompter before this night. One of the first times I ever hosted *Gutfeld!*, I was practicing the monologue and just could not figure out "how I would say" the sentences in front of me, even though I wrote the words, and I *am* me. As I was rehearsing, I got frustrated and wound up telling our executive producer—and, given the fact that I was mic'd up, also the entire control room, all of the panelists, the floor directors, camera guys, etc.—through tears that I was dumb and couldn't do it. Yes, I can be hard on myself. If a Kat Timpf Hot Mic Moment of this incident ever got released, it would be something along the lines of "Hot Mic Reveals Kat Timpf Hates Herself: A Lack of Self-Esteem So Shocking, You Have to Hear It Yourself to Believe It!"

Now, I'm not *crazy* (not certifiably, at least), so I eventually did stop crying, got through the show, and later decided to do something I always *have* been good at: working hard for what I want.

So, I worked on it for hours every day for more than a month, even when I'd rather do anything else. I was getting better!

The next time I hosted, everyone told me how great I'd done, and I honestly believed it was so much better than before. I felt *good*. The next time I hosted, I did it again, same thing. The next time, I didn't mark the scripts, and did just fine then, too.

"See?" everyone said. "We told you, you just had this mental block, and once you got over it, you'd be over it, and it would never happen again."

Until, thanks to Accutane, it did happen again—except it was much, much, much, much worse. A league of its own, really. It left me stuck in my office-cave, unable to face the outside world, full of people who were so much better than I was.

Honestly? Stop what you are doing right now and think of all the people you have called stupid who effortlessly read teleprompters all the time. I can count at least a dozen myself without trying; I know because that is exactly what I did in my head as I was fighting back tears and trying to focus on reading it.

Thinking of all the advice people had given me early on only made me more upset. "Just tell the story like you're talking to me at a bar!" Oh, really? *That's* what I should do? Jesus Christ, hearing that is like hearing someone say if you want to play professional golf you should just get a hole in one every time, except that whenever someone suggested it to me, I actually needed to pretend that it was helpful instead of laughing in their face.

I kept writing:

It is now 10:54 pm, and I am still here because I can't move. I am in a catatonic state; I am really, truly helpless. I mean, at least the hooker knew what she had to do to solve her no-meth problem—but unfortunately for me, you can't dick-suck your way out of incompetence.

Well, there is one other reason, too: I really do look like that hooker, and I really don't want to run into anyone exiting the building looking like this. Worst of all, I can't find any makeup remover, so my best bet really is to wait until I start crying again so that I can wash the rest off with my tears. The only problem is I might be too dehydrated to cry more—a combination of, I'm sure, the Accutane and the fact that it's not like I can go get myself some water looking like this, either.

Incompetence. Failure. The thoughts I have here now, unfortunately, aren't just that I can't read a prompter. They're that my prompter failure defines me. The talents that I do have are a waste and so am I.

Rereading this now, my thought is probably very similar to yours: *Jesus Christ, Kat. Get a grip. Lock it the fuck up!*

Now that I'm off what is, at least for me, the absolute worst drug to ever do, my thoughts then seem absurd. But I share them for a few reasons: First, as I'm sure you know by now, I pride myself on being very good at not judging the whole of another person based on one single statement, belief, or association, because I can see so clearly that, when we do, we miss out on things that could be otherwise meaningful or helpful or even fun. I can see it's not fair; I can see how it's holding us back. I know people are complex, not defined by any one single thing, let alone a mistake or weakness. So much so that I wrote this book! But I want to be clear that, despite all that (and, very especially, thank you to Accutane), I know how it feels to not show that grace to myself. I share this so that if you read it and have felt this way, you can know you're not the only one. I share this because I'm happy to report that things are much, much better now. I'd eventually reach out to Fox and ask if I could get some coaching on the teleprompter, and thanks to advice from my coach and my practice at home, I've already gotten so, so, *so* much better at it—conversational even!—than I was even *before* the Accutane-related meltdown. The elimination of the Accutane has also thankfully restored my sanity to a level where, even if I *hadn't* achieved this strengthening of my skills, I still wouldn't have reacted in such a deranged, despondent way. But I am mainly sharing this—yes, despite the fact that Fox News executives might read it, and I don't think you're supposed to admit any career weaknesses publicly ever, even if you did overcome them, especially if they involve feeling unhinged, let alone to do so in print, and then what if they *really* might not want to let me guest-host on *The Five* ever again— because I want to make clear the contrast between how I was actually feeling and how the audience assumed I was feeling during this time.

See, Cam wasn't the only one who noticed that things with me were different. Clearly, I was depressed . . . and that showed in my work. It showed during the month and a half that I was on it, and then for about a month after that fateful Timpf Bathroom floor incident while it worked its way out of my system.

And how did some in the audience explain this to themselves, evidenced by the tweets I read about myself during a time when I was already feeling bad enough? Many of them along the lines of: **Kat clearly thinks she's too good for the show. If that's how she feels, she should just quit.**

I'd had enough by the time I received an Instagram message from a woman named Mary Kay (that was the name of the woman, not the name of what some woman was trying to sell me) informing me, **You're starting to get a bit full of yourself,** adding, **Don't like it there? Leave.**

I did something I very rarely do, and that was to reply.

I told her the truth! I told this total stranger that I was "trying my best to come out of a very, very dark time," and that "I was on Accutane for a bit and it put me into a deep depression." I told her that what she saw as a person who felt she was too good for the show was actually a person feeling like the *Earth* was too good for *her.* She was gracious and apologized, and I told her that I forgave her, but asked her to please remember that people on TV are people . . . and you don't know what any one of us might be going through.

Of course, ignorance to what people might be going through applies to far more than just those we see on TV. It applies to all of the strangers we see and judge, like in those headlines that pop up on our phones. I am, again, an unabashed free speech absolutist and would never support any effort to stop anyone from being allowed to speak. I also believe that more speech is always better, and that jokes about everything are okay, so none of that is what I'm talking about here.

What I *am* talking about here is a mindset shift, the need to acknowledge a cultural hypocrisy. Take notice just how backward it is that, despite all our preaching about the importance of mental health, we seem to have no tolerance for a person who is struggling with it if it starts to look a little ugly, *which it almost always does.*

This dearth of forgiveness can impact us, even if we're not the person being canceled. For example: Anyone watching a public railroading who might be dealing with some of the same issues as the person being railroaded might feel that all those hateful comments apply to them, too. Some might even find themselves irrationally obsessed with worry about a railroading of their own. In fact, in June 2022, psychiatrist Lindsay-Rose Dykema wrote in a piece for *Slate* that she was "witnessing a new cultural manifestation of OCD," that is, OCD "centered on fear of cancelation." She gave an example of a guy who was constantly and obsessively checking the internet to see if a mistake from his childhood had somehow become public, "paired with compulsive reassurance-seeking that consumed his time and exhausted those around him." What's more, she added that her colleagues had told her they'd seen fear-of-cancelation manifestations of OCD among *their* clients, too.

Considering complexities and leaving yourself open to nuance aren't helpful only when looking at political issues. They're also, and perhaps even more so, important when looking at people. How can we preach and post about how much Mental Health Matters while also taking part in a society where so many people *do* define others by their mistakes?

A mistake or a struggle doesn't equal a person. There should, of course, be accountability for wrongdoing, but there has to be some kind of path to redemption. Most of us are able to do this in our personal lives. What might be harder, though, is to see that the people we read about in headlines have personal lives, too. At this point, it's gone far beyond parasocial relationships and into the realm of parasocial judges and juries, insisting that a person is irredeemable forever based on a single bad moment or characteristic, despite not knowing what that person is going through, or even knowing a thing about the person at all. Just as the public repudiation of a person can have far-reaching consequences, so can choosing to show grace. For one thing, observing more forgiveness and grace might make all of us more willing to examine ourselves, and perhaps even more likely to admit it when we've done something wrong. Instead of being reflexively defensive, people might spend more time listening. Think about it: If there's no path to redemption anyway, what's the motivation to seek it? People must know that path is there if we want to have any hope of them trying to improve themselves.

There's also the fact that a flaw doesn't mean a person has nothing else to offer. Some of the best people in one way have been deeply messed up in others. An extreme example? Vincent van Gogh was so good at painting that he created some of the most iconic artwork in the world, but so terrible at managing his emotions that he once handled his anger by cutting off his own ear.

It is certainly important for people to show accountability for their actions, but that's exactly what it should be: accountability *for their actions*, not accountability *for their being*. Of course, there will be times that this analysis does show that a person needs to be locked away forever. Ted Bundy, for example! But other times, accountability can be a learning experience, the first step to a new, improved person, which is a truly amazing thing—not only for the sake of that person but also for the sake of what they might be able to offer the rest of us.

One of the best ways to set ourselves up to approach another person's mental health crisis with grace could work wonders in combatting the impulse to so quickly and easily write others off for any reason, and that is: *to get over ourselves.*

It's an unexpected thing to hear from a television personality, I know. And I'm going to tell you what made me realize it, but first, I need to warn you that the sentence you're about to read is going to make you roll your eyes so hard that you might pass out: my weeklong safari trip in Africa.

I know. I know, I know, I know. That is maybe *the* most cringeworthy thing I could have said, maybe just underneath some dude wearing a tapestry as a shirt talking at you about how doing shrooms with his buddy Aiden at Joshua Tree changed his life, man.

But I would encourage you to keep reading—not *even if* you hated me after reading that, but *especially if* you did. Because by the time I'm done, I am going to call myself out even more.

But, yeah, you do have to listen to me talk about Africa first.

As Kyle, a friend of (my friend/colleague) Kennedy's and a South African native who planned our trip, repeatedly pointed out, people who say "Nature is so peaceful" have no idea what they're talking about. It's not peaceful; it's chaos. I came face-to-face with a leopard out there who was known for mating with both a father and son leopard *in front of each other*. That is one wild animal. (Or at the very least, one that's been listening to 2018-era episodes of *Call Her Daddy*.)

I saw lots of things that shocked me. Even parrots shocked me out there. I've seen them in pet stores or whatever, but seeing them out there reminded me that they do exist in the wild, not just as novelty pets for weirdos. The first time I saw one, I thought to myself: *How ridiculous, to wake up every day and you're lime green*. You know? No matter how low-key and chill you might be feeling, if you're a parrot, you're still lime green. Parrots have to be both sad and lime green at the same time! They have to convince other animals to take them seriously while they're lime green. If they wanted to have an emo phase, they'd have to do it lime green. And don't even get me started on how leopards have to wake up wearing animal print. Absurd!

Among the madness, I also saw a lot of things I could relate to human life. For example: A lone male cape buffalo is dangerous. The way our guide explained it to us, the animal is going to be angry and agitated—not only because of whatever *reason* he's alone, but also because he *is* alone. Exactly like male humans! It's not just Reddit; the African wilderness has incels too!

There were a lot of places to find inspiration, too. Like, I'm so scared of being able to maintain a career and be a mom at the same time, but lionesses do it—and stalking and killing a wildebeest is a way harder job than getting your hair and makeup done and saying what's on your mind. I'm also guessing it's a lot harder, and certainly higher stakes, to search for a good hiding spot for your young so you can go hunt than it is to go search for adequate childcare to go to your cable news job.

Speaking of scared! There were definitely a few times when I thought that I might die. We had more in common with the antelope—that is, the bottom animals on the food chain—than any of the other creatures. I mean, yeah, we were in a safari vehicle, which I logically knew made things pretty safe, and our guide had a gun, but still. We're also slower, and, unlike the antelope, we were *paying* to be there. If any of those antelope knew that, I'm sure they would talk to each other about how dumb we all were. I thought about that a lot. One evening, our tour guide and animal tracker left with the rifle to look for a nearby rhino on foot, leaving us tourists alone in the open safari vehicle. Then suddenly, I hear Kyle say, all matter-of-fact-like: "Oh, look, there's the rhino." No big deal, just, "Oh, the rhino," and I'm like, *It's a fucking rhino; I am going to die*, because I have never in my life been in that kind of situation before. I later figured that Kyle's calm versus my fear was probably similar to how someone visiting New York City from out of town might freak out the first time a bum screams in their face. Like, New Yorkers understand in those situations what Kyle understood in this one: This may be wild . . . but it won't, at least usually, end in your death.

All of *my* skills are useless in the African bush. Well, I mean, sure, I was able to make the tour guides laugh. Our guide, Trico, is a staunch opponent of PC culture. He laughed as he told us a very funny story about how he was supposed to bring a guest something but got sidetracked, and then later got to overhear from around a corner as the guest struggled to describe him to someone else because he didn't want to say that Trico was black. We talked about *South Park* together, and Amber Heard. Later, when he was describing how wildebeest defecate to mark their territory, I exclaimed: "Oh, but when *Amber Heard* does it, it's a problem!"

While I was out there, I just kept thinking about how much time I've spent freaking out about work, or if that email I sent was okay, or if so-and-so was mad at me—and meanwhile, across the world there are antelopes freaking out that they're about to be mauled to death every time they hear a twig break . . . *which is all the damn time.*

There really is nothing quite so humbling as being surrounded by dozens of elephants and realizing: *Hey, it's actually* not *up to me whether I live or die right now.*

Perhaps the loudest, clearest lesson was the one I'm also the most afraid to write about for fear of being canceled—and, yes, I am saying this even after I have known what it is like to fear being canceled as in, literally trampled by an angry herd of elephants.

But here it is anyway: I went to Africa during the last week of October 2023, a particularly tragic news week. It was just weeks after Hamas's brutal attack on Israel; between the war in the Middle East and a mass shooting in Maine, there was so much tragedy that *Gutfeld!* was preempted multiple times.

Being in Africa during that time was illuminating because, well, no one there was talking about any of it. It was enlightening *not* because I somehow realized all of it was not as tragic as I would have thought otherwise, because of course it is. It was more so personally witnessing what I'd always known but never really been confronted by firsthand: There is lots of tragedy around the world all the time, whether the U.S. media decides to focus on it or not. It sounds trite and maybe it is, but some of that was as simple as seeing the less fortunate and being grateful for what I have. My time out in Africa, after all, was spent in a *very* privileged way, going on two safaris at two different parks, and let me tell you: The car ride between the two made me not only know, but have to also actually see, just how good I had it. To be clear: I am not congratulating myself for this, because the way it makes me feel is actually the opposite of laudable, and exactly how the safari itself made me feel: small, unimportant, and quite frankly ridiculous for having ever felt any other way.

It's not that it's wrong to mourn tragedy. That's what separates humans from monsters. But let's be real with ourselves for a second: It's also not as though Mourning Tragedy would be the best description of the conversations I saw among members of the media and politicians as I was scrolling my phone between safaris. Rather, a lot of it was comprised of people melting down over who had what Bad Take on a tragic thing, as well as celebrating the people who chastised the Bad Takes as heroes for having done so. (I know, I said "scrolling my phone between safaris." Gag me, I'm the worst.)

In any case, the United States in general—and even more so, the American media specifically—is not the complete center of the whole world's universe the way that our attitudes often indicate, and I myself am even less so. The illusion is exactly that.

Being real with ourselves about our insignificance is *so* illuminating, and employing it could go a long way—especially given a lot of what we see people say regarding mental health on social media. I don't mean just the blatantly idiotic stuff, like the Wellness Coach Moms on Instagram who post things like *If you want to kill yourself, try having a glass of water first!* And then there's a link to branded water bottles that say "HYDRATION NOT SUICIDAL IDEATION," or the Red Pill Edgelord Dads on Twitter/X who rake in ad revenue with the rage they incite by posting things like *Depression isn't real, you just need to go to the gym and impregnant your tradwife, libtards.*

Rather than talking about what's (hopefully) obviously stupid, I'd rather question what's seemingly unquestioned: the narrative that *the* way to mass happiness is to convince each of us to be passionately in love with ourselves.

Amid an internet full of pink-glitter PSAs telling us that we're all *so* special and *so* amazing and "Just in case no one told you today, you are exactly where you need to be and your butt looks amazing," reminders that, actually, each of us is pretty *unimportant* could go a long way in making all of us better people.

A 2015 study published in the *Journal of Personality and Social Psychology* found that feelings of awe—you know, the kind of feelings you get on a safari in Africa—made people feel "small," prompting them to be more generous and compassionate.

It makes sense! When you think you're perfect, after all, you're going to be a lot less compelled to show grace toward a person demonstrating the horrifying ugliness of a breakdown. When you recognize that you're a but a blip in a wide wilderness, you'll feel a lot less qualified in condemning someone else, let alone congratulating yourself for doing it.

Again, I know all of this might seem strange coming from a person who Does Hot Takes for a Living, but it's not that I'm not saying our viewpoints aren't worth sharing, or that our lives aren't worth appreciating, because of course they are. I'm just saying we should also remember not to get so caught up in ourselves that we can't see beyond that—not only for the sake of others' mental health but also for our own.

7

Taxation Is Armed Robbery

I agreed to be a guest on Bill Maher's *Club Random* podcast at the last minute, filling the spot of someone else who had dropped out, during what was already one of the busiest weeks of my life—so busy it would have been impossible to manage if I weren't one of those people who are kind of addicted to chaos. I'm sure it's not healthy, but I guess I've just always seen it as a tantalizing alternative to that paralyzing emptiness I can feel whenever things calm down enough for my brain to deem them "boring."

My first book had come out the previous week, and I'd been doing nonstop press and promotion. I loved talking about the contents of my book, apart from the constant fear that I was doing it wrong. I really, really, *really* wanted people to read it; the subject was *so* important, and I'd been careful to nail the execution—sometimes even spending an hour or more editing a single sentence or two, inspired by the way one of my favorite authors, John Updike, was able to write such perfect little passages in his Rabbit novels that many of them have stuck with me my entire life. (Yeah, that bit about hate as a shelter isn't the only one that's stuck with me; there are *so* many: "We do survive every moment, after all, except the last one." "How can you respect the world when you see it's being run by a bunch of kids turned old?" "It comes to him: growth is betrayal. There is no other route. There is no arriving somewhere without leaving somewhere." "Rabbit realized the world was not solid and benign, it was a shabby set of temporary arrangements rigged up for the time being, all for the sake of money." "We are cruel enough without meaning to be." "You can't trust anybody not to fuck." And then there's the one that made me sob over and over again after my mom died: "What you lose as you age is witnesses, the ones that watched from early on and cared, like your own little grandstand." *Ouch*.)

Anyway, I really believed *You Can't Joke About That* was the best thing I'd ever done—like, so much so that I worried I might not even be able to put "the best thing I've ever done" in an Instagram caption celebrating my future hypothetical child's hypothetical first birthday—and one of very few things I'd ever felt this kind of confidence about. I'm far more inclined to doubt my own work than to like it, let alone think that other people would like it, too.

I was proud because I knew the book could resonate with anyone. It was a human book about human stuff, not a political book about political stuff, but I was also worried that people might think the opposite when they saw that it was a Fox News author's book. You know? Some people might assume that it was about The Woke Left Ruining Comedy and not read it because they didn't want to read a book about that, but it *wasn't* a book about that; it had only one chapter about politics, and it hit both sides. But were people going to see "Fox News" and think that my place of employment told them everything they needed to know? Was this an impossible uphill battle, and nothing I could do would ever be good enough to accomplish what I was going for? And do you see what I mean about the self-doubt?

As for the explicitly promotional "Pick up a copy!" "Available now on Amazon!" part of the process, I wanted to crawl out of my skin the entire time. Like . . . "Hello, everyone! It's me! Want more of me? Hell ya you do, please buy hundreds of pages of my thoughts and opinions!!" Like, *shoot* me in the *mouth*, you know? It drove me nuts to see any comment from anyone saying it was annoying for me to be promoting my book so much, because all of them were assuming I didn't totally agree!

My schedule had me in four cities in four states within five days: New York City for my regular job, *Gutfeld!*, on Monday; a speech in Athens, Georgia, on Tuesday; *Club Random* in Los Angeles on Wednesday; back to NYC for *Gutfeld!* Thursday and Friday; then to Chicago on Saturday for the very first live show of my tour on Sunday.

There were a lot of crazy moments: messing up the booking of my hair and makeup several times, ordering Chinese food to Wisconsin instead of to Georgia—and, of course, sitting in a car with my friend and knowing that it was headed to Maher's property, where he would want (or at least have been convinced he *should* want) to talk to me.

I was totally freaking out about where I was going. Not about what I'd say in the interview, but about whether or not I'd smoke the weed I'd seen Maher smoking with some of his other guests on the podcast. Yes, seriously: My anxiety is as terrible in frequency as it is at choosing what's worth being anxious about, to the point that I've wondered whether it could be a defense mechanism of some kind. Like, maybe my brain has figured out that, since I absolutely *am* going to sweat, it's best that I *do* sweat the small stuff, regardless of what the motivational posters say, because at least then I could assure myself of how small the stuff was to calm myself down. Think about it: If I'm freaking out about whether I should accept weed, then I can tell myself how dumb it is to be freaking out about whether I should accept weed, because that *is* dumb—thereby convincing myself that I have Nothing to Worry About. Rather than, you know, confront the reality that I did have something to worry about: I was about to be interviewed by an extremely rich, extremely famous, extremely influential man whom I'd been watching on TV since college, and it would be the first time a whole new audience would be seeing me, and I had better not fuck all of that up. (Note: As is so often the case with things that I concern-spiral about, it never happened. I wasn't offered weed at any point; it never came up.)

The property was huge. I waited in the greenroom building, complete with a deck overlooking some kind of duck pond while Maher interviewed Mayim Bialik in the studio. I checked to make sure all my reminder alarms (ADHD Life!) were turned off. (As anyone who watched the interview would know, I somehow did this wrong. A loud, car horn ringtone alarm would go off toward the end of the podcast anyway, and he would scold me, and I would scold *myself* well into the future on those nights when my brain decides that scolding me for things that happened ages ago is a bigger priority than sleep.) Now that it seemed weed wouldn't be an option, I focused on how I couldn't decide how much to drink. There was a ton of alcohol in the greenroom, and I knew we'd be drinking during the podcast, too. I ultimately decided to do a small shot of tequila with my friend and then nurse a Michelob Ultra, the same one that I would eventually carry with me to the studio for the interview.

I got mic'd up and we sat down and just started talking. No one let me know when the filming started. It just starts as soon as you sit down, and no one warns you about that ahead of time. I was kind of nervous at first, I guess, because well, it's Bill Maher. I wouldn't say I was starstruck, necessarily, because the vibe of the whole thing was far too comfortable to feel that way. Kind of like how it must feel to see what you were told ahead of time was an alien from outer space, but who wound up being so totally chill that you kept forgetting he wasn't just some guy from Pittsburgh. Like, you've *seen* what they look like according to various media, but, now that you're face-to-face with one, he's just offering you drinks as you chat casually with him about topics ranging from booze to your nine frozen embryos to anal sex to abortion to your dead mother. All those topics went quite smoothly. Almost too smoothly. I was at times concerned my comfort level with certain topics might give some people the vibe that I'm Not a Lady. (Okay, so I know I'm irreverent, and also pretty open, including about things that are embarrassing or crude, and that doesn't bother me about myself. Actually? I *like* those things about me. Still, after I've shared things that are vulnerable or "vulgar," especially on a podcast or in a book, I'll often immediately feel so anxious about facing judgment for saying them—especially since women are judged far more harshly for irreverence, or even a lack of politeness, real or perceived, than men are.) The vibe of the conversation shifted once, and only once, when we started talking about taxes.

We'd just been talking about how Maher was so rich that he was able to just allow one of his pools to become a duck pond—because some ducks started hanging out there and he liked them and he had another pool anyway, so why not let them live there—and how that differs from my rental apartment and how expensive it is to have luxuries like a baby or a place to put a baby in New York City.

Kat: I don't believe in taxes because I think it's armed robbery.
Bill: You must believe in some taxes.
Kat: I don't actually.
Bill: Oh, that's so stupid.
Kat: I don't actually. It's stupid? That's okay. But can you agree that it's immoral, though?

Then he called me "stupid" more, to which I said, "It's immoral to take someone's money without their consent," and then he told me I should move to Somalia because there're no taxes there and it's lawless and there are "gangs and militias who fight each other and terrorize the population because they don't have money from taxes." He went on to say there were "parts" of his "philosophy" he "would label as libertarian, which is people should be able to do whatever they want as long as it doesn't hurt somebody else," but that, although the government does waste money, "you can't live in a functional society without taxes," making what I was saying "intensely stupid."

"I'm not talking about policy though; do you know what I'm saying?" I said, still completely calm and as cool as the Michelob Ultra I was clutching in my right hand.

He did say that they take "too much money," but that was only because we were "on Earth, where life is not perfect," adding that, despite calling me stupid so many times, he was "pissed off at taxes too."

I took a giant swig of my beer before I decided to pivot to joking around: "Is there a duck pond tax? Because now you've changed my mind. Now I'm super Left-wing, now I'm a socialist, and I look at your pool with the ducks in it and I'm like, 'You know what? I own this pool now; this is a government pool.'"

His face *lit the fuck up* when I mentioned the ducks, leading me to then ask him if the ducks had names . . . because I knew judging by his face that they absolutely did have names. He told me that their names were "Onyx" and "Ducky," and they, as he put it, "came into my life about six months ago." He had all the excitement of a CrossFit guy after you'd asked him about his workout routine (minus the aggression and the weirdness of having some kind of hero complex for something you're paying to do in a gym) and all the adorableness of a kid showing me he'd just lost his first tooth.

A few things about how this conversation went down stuck with me: For one, the guy who had just been repeatedly calling me "stupid" in our conversation about taxes was so quick and willing to share something personal with me. It's exactly what I hope this book might demonstrate: Even when we vociferously disagree on divisive political issues, there are millions of other things that can, and should, unite us.

But I'd also like to discuss how this whole thing was an example of what we seem to do all too readily: miss each other's points. For me, I hadn't really meant to bring up any sort of policy debate. In my mind, I was sharing an objective truth: Whether you love taxes or hate taxes or fall somewhere in the middle, you really can't deny that they are anything but theft.

Think about it this way: Instead of using the word "government," let's just say "Sam." You work hard, make money, and then Sam takes a ton of it from you and you have to give it to him or else a bunch of people who work for Sam will show up at your house with guns, bust down your door, and lock you in a cage for years because you didn't pay him. What else is that *but* armed robbery?

Not to mention the fact that Sam spends that money on some really messed-up stuff sometimes, like the wars I discussed in my "Half-Veteran" chapter, forcing taxpayers like me who oppose those wars to pay for them anyway. Sam also funded research at the Wuhan virology lab that very well may have (according to many experts, multiple government agencies, and, in my view, common sense) leaked the virus that killed millions of people worldwide, and doesn't have to face consequences for any of it. Oh, and then there's this: In an attempt to stop a virus from spreading, Sam might also ban you from operating your business, not caring that that's how you make money to feed your family, ultimately causing you to lose that business entirely, and face no consequences for *that*, either. If you're not angry yet, think about it this way: Whatever percentage the government takes from your income in taxes, that's the percentage of the year that you're working without compensation. For example, if you're taxed at 50 percent, you're working for six months out of each year for free.

Any association of taxation with altruism feels a bit gaslight-y, especially considering that many of taxation's most fervent warriors in terms of words don't seem to apply the same passion when it comes to paying theirs.

For example, in 2019, Minnesota Rep. Ilhan Omar made headlines for suggesting tax rates "as high as 90 percent" as "a place we can start," because "[t]he one percent must pay their fair share," calling any opposition to this idea (you guessed it!) "a problem of moral courage."

Months later, Omar made headlines again—this time because Minnesota campaign finance investigators revealed that she'd filed joint tax returns with her now-husband before they were married and while she was married to someone else, a violation of both state and federal law. (For the record, the AP reports that Omar emailed them a statement saying, "All of Rep. Omar's tax filings are fully compliant with all applicable tax law," adding that she'd said in another statement the week prior that she would comply with the board's filings, including paying a penalty.)

Then there's New York Rep. Alexandria Ocasio-Cortez, Omar's fellow Squad member, who loves to talk about taxes. Remember that "TAX THE RICH" dress she wore to the 2021 Met Gala? In 2020, the *New York Post* reported she had an outstanding seven-year-old tax bill from a failed business (AOC's camp said the bill was issued in error). To make it, pun intended, even more rich: Aurora James, AOC's dress designer—the one AOC touted as a "working class" "woman immigrant designer"— was an immigrant from fucking *Canada*, coming to the United States *not* from war-torn Somalia or Third World Honduras, but a suburb of Toronto. Even funnier? James was later branded as a "notorious tax deadbeat" by the *New York Post* after it alleged that her LLC had been hit with fifteen open tax warrants since 2015, and that, despite allegedly receiving $41,666 in taxpayer-funded pandemic relief money, James purchased a $1.6 million home in Los Angeles in September 2020.

(Come to think of it, many of the people demanding massive tax increases, who insist it's immoral to oppose them, who would call me an asshole for being upset about the amount that I pay in them, would also be the first ones to dump on me for the way that I make most of the money that they take—that is, by working at Fox News. Yes, the same people who would call me an irredeemable wretch for my work sure have a lot of ideas for the money that I make doing it. As many of my fellow cringe millennials have said before me: Make it make sense!)

Anyway, it's not just members of Congress hypocritically chastising us about paying our "fair share," either. For example, President Joe Biden! He declared: "Look, we've got a better answer. It's time for everyone—I mean everyone, no matter how rich or powerful they are—to start paying their fair share." That's a precious declaration. Especially because it came in June 2023, just days after his own son, Hunter, was about to admit to not paying taxes on taxable income over $1.5 million in 2017–18 as part of a plea deal that later fell apart.

In general, the "fair share" idea amounts to narcissism and entitlement; so it's pretty backward that opposing this thinking has somehow been branded as the selfish viewpoint. Who are you to determine what your "fair share" of my money is? Especially since a lot of the people I hear it from don't exactly seem to hate having money themselves.

The most obvious example, of course, would be democratic socialist Bernie Sanders, a guy who, as I mentioned earlier, never shuts up about the evils of The Rich while he owns multiple homes and is estimated to be worth multiple millions.

But he's not the only one.

In January 2023, then–House Speaker Nancy Pelosi, owner of the infamous $24,000 fridge, slammed Republicans for wanting to "let wealthy tax cheats off the hook," even though her name, to many a middle-class American, is synonymous with "wealthy" and "cheat." Pelosi's net worth, according to several estimates, is roughly in the triple-digit millions range, most of which comes from her venture-capitalist husband. Regardless of the source or estimated range, Pelosi still has a lot more money than you—I mean, I'm guessing; if I'm wrong, please buy two or three books—or I will ever have. Pelosi claims she "absolutely" never gave her husband, Paul, any tips that informed his stock trades, but in my opinion a lot of his actions suggest otherwise. For example, dumping 30,000 shares of Google stock in December 2022, just weeks before the Department of Justice filed an antitrust lawsuit against the company. Or in March 2022, when Paul scooped up $5 million worth of Tesla stock as Pelosi pushed for subsidies on electric cars. Or March 2021, when Paul bought 25,000 shares in Microsoft, valued at more than $5 million, just a little more than a week before the army announced a contract to buy Microsoft's virtual reality headsets, a $22 billion contract that spiked the value of those shares. Those aren't even all the examples, but I don't want you to get as bored as I am examining her vast wealth. Moreover, I trust you're smart enough to already see the point: The Pelosis did nothing wrong, and Paul is just a really good guesser!

In my view? To use Bill Maher's favorite word, you'd have to be "stupid" to believe that.

It's not just the Pelosis doing shady stuff, either. There's also North Carolina Republican and then–Senate Intelligence Committee chairman Richard Burr, a dude with more access to information about the pandemic than the average American, publicly assuring Americans in February 2020 that COVID-19 was nothing to worry about, while he himself was dumping hundreds of thousands of dollars in stocks, including in the hospitality industry (which would obviously struggle when politicians would later make the whole industry essentially illegal in the name of COVID-19). Burr also hit up his brother-in-law, a member of the National Mediation Board, who dumped a bunch of his stocks just minutes after their call. When news of all this broke, Burr stepped down as the chair of the intelligence committee—however, unlike what I believe would happen if it were you or I, neither man was charged with a crime. (For the record: Both men, of course, denied that they'd done anything wrong.)

Here's another stat that should grind your taxpaying gears: A *New York Times* analysis published in September 2022 "found that 97 lawmakers or their family members bought or sold financial assets over a three-year span in industries that could be affected by their legislative committee work."

As *Daily Beast* journalist Matt K. Lewis, author of *Filthy Rich Pol-*

iticians: The Swamp Creatures, Latte Liberals, and Ruling-Class Elites Cashing in on America, told the *Guardian*: "Rich people get elected, and people, when elected, tend to get richer. Over time, it has gotten worse . . . I think it's just an irony that I wrote the book *Filthy Rich Politicians* in a moment when all the politicians in America . . . one thing almost all have in common is trying to position themselves as being populist outsiders attacking elites," he said.

It's ironic. It's absurd. And it's everywhere.

To be clear: I'm not a hater for no reason, and I do think that it's quite impressive to go from being a bartender to being in Congress, as AOC did, and I've always thought it was pretty gross to see people dump on her for that. For one thing, weren't our politicians supposed to be normal people? For another, I can relate to that upward mobility, albeit on a smaller scale, going from Boston Market cashier to a regular on one of the biggest cable news networks. I, too, sometimes see people attacking me for not having The Qualifications to be in my position, and it drives me insane. Honestly, not enough people realize that sometimes becoming a person with a PhD is the result of being a person with little direction and a lot of family money. Some people go to college simply because, as Shaun puts it in American movie masterpiece *Orange County*, "It's what you do after high school." You weren't sure what to major in, but you loved to read, so you picked English. Then, after you graduated, you still didn't know what to do, so you just went back to school for your master's. Then, you still didn't know what to do, so you decided to get a PhD in Chaucer or something. I don't mean to diminish the accomplishment—yes, it *is* impressive, and no, not everyone could do it, but there are a lot of people out there who could do it, at least intelligence-wise, but didn't, because they lacked either the cash or the aimlessness. I see myself as one of those people! I got into an Ivy League grad school; I even enrolled. The only reason I didn't go was because I didn't have $80,000 and I didn't think it would be smart to borrow $80,000 without any reason to think I'd be able to pay it back. AOC being a bartender says nothing about her intelligence and, sometimes, neither does a lack of degrees. This is especially true in the age of the internet, when all of us have so much information at our fingertips, carrying little supercomputers in our pockets with us everywhere we go, allowing us to educate ourselves. Far too many people, instead of educating themselves, apparently prefer to instead remain in a partisan bubble . . . using their pocket supercomputer only to tell people in other bubbles that they're ugly or fat or racist or pedophiles or whatever, but I digress.

One of the many differences between AOC and me is that I not only understand but also acknowledge that my current life is a manifestation of capitalism. For instance, I can recognize as the owner of a French bulldog (like AOC as well!) that these dogs, the most popular breed in the United States in 2022 and 2023, wouldn't even be a thing without capitalism. There's a reason you rarely see them chortling around in the streets of the Dominican Republic when you're on your way from the airport to your all-inclusive resort. They're a designer breed; they don't reproduce by themselves; they're all the products of IUI—a fertility treatment many only wish they could afford to aid themselves in having human babies. Then, the puppies all have to be delivered via C-section, because their heads are too big for them to be birthed naturally. All French bulldogs aside, I've always thought that expressing support for capitalism garners inordinate accusations of cruelty considering that market-based systems have lifted more people out of poverty than any other system in the world's history. In any case, wealth in Congress is hardly a rarity in *either* party; this has been the case for a long time. According to a *Quartz* piece from 2018, the median U.S. Congress member in 2015 was worth twelve times more than the median American *household*, adding that these were also "conservative estimates." They were generally unaffected by the 2008–09 financial crisis, too: "Since 2006, while the median congress person continued to get richer, the typical American household saw their wealth decline, dented by the 2008–09 financial crisis."

While Democrats are the ones who most often wax poetic about the moral value of taxes, hypocritical given everything I've just explained, Republicans prefer to wax poetic about taxes being bad with their words—hypocritical, given some of their actions.

In April 2023, Republicans advanced debt-ceiling legislation that would have, as the *Wall Street Journal* noted, hiked taxes by "hundreds of billions" over ten years. But Republicans touted the legislation as a good thing, because it would have minimized initiatives such as Biden administration environmental subsidies.

"We know that these green-energy policies that the Biden administration has forced down the throat of Americans is not good for this country," Georgia Republican Rep. Drew Ferguson said about the bill, the Limit, Save, Grow Act of 2023. "It's not good for American competitiveness, and I really don't care what the CBO score is. What I care about is doing the right thing."

Did you catch that? Yes, this bill would raise taxes, but ultimately, by getting rid of that nasty Green Stuff, they were "doing the right thing"? In other words: They were making the exact same moral argument as the Democrats, but in a roundabout way: Yes, this bill raises taxes, but it is good because of the *moral value* of what it does—ignoring that, ultimately, their version of "morality" often amounts to nothing other than "something that I can brand as 'morality' in order to score points with my base," stealing money from their constituents for their own political ends.

The bill never had any hope of passing the Democrat-controlled Senate, but still, its passage in the Republican-controlled House, according to the same *WSJ* piece, "shows Republicans are less focused on official tax tallies and more determined to reverse Mr. Biden's agenda."

The *WSJ* piece continues:

> Republicans can tell their supporters at home that they are
> reversing Mr. Biden's energy policies, a move that could assuage

voters worried about increasing federal revenue, said Sage
Eastman, a former House GOP tax aide.

Not all tax cuts are created equal any more.

Unfortunately, at this point, the difference between the parties on
taxation is one of pure semantics. At this point, Republicans are not
anti-taxation so much as they are anti-Democrat. Republicans as the
"fiscally responsible" party is more ruse than reality and has been for
years. So much of the spending hikes, after all, were the product of the
Bush administration's wars. (Reread my "Half-Veteran" chapter if you
need a reminder of how worth it *that* stuff was. Short version: It wasn't,
except for maybe if your dad's on the board of Lockheed Martin.)

Not to mention that high taxes are due to high spending, and,
although Republicans may talk about cutting spending, it doesn't always work out that way. For example: In the spring of 2016, Trump
claimed he could pay down the entire national debt in just eight years.
Although he has yet, of course, to actually serve eight years, the time
that he did serve strongly suggests that this wouldn't be the case. In
just the first three years of his presidency (including two when Republicans controlled the White House, House, and Senate) federal spending *increased* $900 billion—the same increase we saw under Obama's
entire eight-year presidency. The same amount of spending in less than
half the time, and this was before the pandemic!

When it comes to taxes, both sides have one main thing in common, something that transcends whatever differences they may have:
They determine how they'll talk about them based on their political
goals rather than reality. They aren't going to stop doing that, because
they aren't going to campaign against their own power.

So, it's up to us to bring reality into the conversation. Calling these
things what they are is the only way we can be sure we're talking about
what really is, and it's important for us to do that, regardless of our view

on how good we think they are for society—which is the point I was trying to make when I was talking to Maher. In many cases, refusing to blindly accept government language provides a check on government power, which is important not in spite of the Greater Good, but precisely because of it. Put another way, it's easier for the government to get away with things if the rest of us are speaking about whatever it does on *its* terms. I mean, if you count my job at a pizza shop when I was in high school (which you should, cleaning dishes in the back to get away from your convict manager making comments about how your ass looks in your jeans when you're just sixteen years old is definitely work), I've been paying taxes for about twenty years now. During that time, I've paid for pointless wars, gain-of-function research, the imprisonment of people because they were caught with the wrong plant—countless examples of places my money has gone that not only fail to meet the government's standard of "making our lives better," but many actively making lives worse, or even ending lives entirely.

There's also this: If we unquestionably and thoughtlessly accept and employ the language of the powerful, and we accept the unrealistic definitions given to us by people who have a motivation to manipulate them, we are going to hate each other for reasons that aren't even real. It's easy to hate someone for criticizing taxation, especially if you believe that indicates they don't care about the sick, the poor, or anyone else who is struggling.

But one opinion does not automatically indicate the other. Sure, there are people who are greedy. I know what greed is; I've seen *Billy Madison*. (FU, Eric Gordon!) But for me, and so many others, it's not that I wouldn't gladly give money to help solve those problems—because I would. I just don't think the government spends the money it takes from us with the Needs of the People in mind so much as how the special interest groups and/or war machine want them to spend it—because people in power want to stay there.

Taxation is just one example, but there are many instances of how government language pits us against each other unnecessarily: Calling it "student loan cancelation" or "student loan forgiveness" makes people who oppose it sound like jerks for not wanting to simply get rid of struggling people's debt, but really, it's *not* "forgiveness" or "cancelation" at all; it's the coercive reassignment of payments to people who had nothing to do with them. Or, there's the way that people use "health care" and "health insurance" interchangeably, suggesting that anyone opposed to, for example, single-payer government health *insurance* is actually opposed to people receiving health *care*, when the two are entirely different things. In general, it's important to realize that not believing that the government is the way to solve a problem is *not* the same as not caring about it.

We shouldn't let the government's branding campaign—so often nothing but a tool used to prop up its own power while its members enrich themselves—become a reason for us to hate each other. If you want to hate someone for being greedy or selfish, then that's one thing. Just make sure that your assessment is based in reality first—and not influenced by inaccurate language that might have twisted your brain into inaccurate assumptions. Or else you might, for example, end up calling a person "stupid," when she's actually astute enough to realize how badly you want to talk about your ducks.

8

"Think of the Children!"

I don't mind when horrible things happen to children. I don't care if they're groomed sexually, get addicted to vaping or drugs, die in school shootings, or kill themselves. It's kind of whatever to me.

If reading that shocked you? Good, it should. Those would be horrific things to believe—so horrific, in fact, that it's difficult to even imagine a person feeling that way. Here's the thing, though: People often act differently when discussing politics.

Of course I care when bad things happen to kids. *Of course* I don't want them to be sexually abused, or murdered, or on drugs. That's not exactly a brag, either. The same way it's not a brag to not meet the DSM-5 definition for psychopathy.

The only thing more absurd than the argument itself might be how commonly we see people throw it around, suggesting people don't treat it as absurd at all.

It does us no good and tears us apart unnecessarily. Granted, the only reason we keep seeing it is that it does work great for politicians, government, and (other) grifters.

In the summer of 2020, things were *preeeeetty* contentious. There was that whole pandemic thing, there was that whole George Floyd thing. A lot of us were locked in our houses, faced with the dangerous combination of having more time than ever to drink heavily, few options but the internet for human connection, *and* the highest risk of being canceled for drunkenly saying the wrong thing online. The bar was never lower for earning the label of "grandma killer." You used to have to kill a grandma to get called that! But in the summer of 2020, all you had to do was go to a restaurant, or just say that it should be legal to go to a restaurant. People were sick, people were dying, schools were closed, businesses were being destroyed, and our government managed to find bipartisan support to do *what*, of all things?

Ban flavored Juul pods.

I tweeted that July: **Our government may not be sure how to handle this pandemic but at least they can agree that I must not be allowed to obtain a mango-flavored Juul pod.**

Why? The Kids, obviously.

I was angry about this at the time. That may be a slight understatement, considering that a mere two days later I again took to Twitter/X: **I'm serious. Can anyone mail me some mango Juul pods from somewhere you can still find them? I will do anything up to and including killing your wife.** I even trekked up to the Bronx in their pursuit. See, at the time, I was *very* addicted to vaping, and had a strong preference for the exact flavors the government and other anti-vaping advocates insisted on banning on behalf of The Kids.

I was *beyond* addicted, actually. Vaping was part of my identity: My Twitter was full of jokes about it. (**I would be terrible on *Naked and Afraid*. My partner would be like hi I'm Dustin I am a survival coach and my one chosen item is an ax to build shelter and I'd be like hi I'm Kat I do a ten-minute ab video three times a week and my one chosen item is my vape.**) I was notorious for asking bartenders and Uber drivers to plug mine in, sometimes choosing to charge my vape over charging my phone. I once publicly requested that, in lieu of incense, there be a procession of people vaping at my funeral. I'd ripped my vape, which I affectionally referred to as my "e-skag," on Fox News and during Barstool News Network's 2016 election coverage. A fan named a very strong vape liquid after me, and was right on point for having chosen that concentration level: When a dental procedure once prohibited me from vaping for twenty-four hours, the withdrawal was so bad that I covered myself in enough nicotine patches to kill a normal human, or at least make her throw up and pass out, and I didn't even feel a *buzz*.

The push to ban the pods came after roughly a year of hearing reports about kids dying from vaping, allegedly including from vaping nicotine. Of course it's *horrific* that children were dying. I shouldn't even have to say that. Or, rather, I shouldn't have felt like I had to say it, because I probably didn't really need to, because I'm sure you already know that I think that, or you would never have bought this book, because who would want to buy a book from a monster?

To me, however, the narrative just didn't add up. For one thing, I'd been blowing fruity-flavored clouds every waking moment of every day for years, and yet I was still somehow very much alive—was I the, like, *Keith Richards* of vaping, with my very survival being a medical marvel? Or was the prevailing narrative missing the truth?

(To be clear, although I have seen that Public Health England study estimating vaping as 95 percent safer than cigarettes, I also knew that vaping, especially at the level I was doing it, probably wasn't *healthy* for me, which is why I stopped on September 12, 2022. Well, that and the fact that I felt like, if I wound up with lung cancer, I would feel really stupid, which is probably the last thing you want to feel when you're already feeling cancer.)

For another thing, instead of just accepting that nicotine vapes were slaughtering children, or being too afraid to question if they were because kids were involved, I'd already been researching the issue for months. What's more, my research revealed that the prevailing narrative was a lot different from the actual science. As I explained in an article for *National Review* in January 2020:

According to the CDC, the vast majority of the illnesses and deaths were due to THC vaping products—particularly those that had been obtained on the black market—containing Vitamin E acetate. In fact, when I spoke with Carrie Wade (the director of harm-reduction policy at the R Street Institute, who also has an educational background in neuroscience and pharmacology), she told me that "it would surprise" her if "any" of the illnesses or deaths were due to nicotine. She said that she believed that people who admitted only to vaping nicotine might simply be "hesitant to admit" that they had been using a marijuana product as well, especially if they were teens—because, due to the difference in the chemical properties of nicotine from those of THC, she "doesn't see a need for the problematic type of chemical to be in a nicotine product" at all.

Considering that the problem here was black-market products, banning the legal ones could clearly do more harm than good by potentially pushing more people to that exact market. My research had also debunked some of the other reasoning behind the ban (fewer than 6 percent of teenagers, including adults, were addicted to vaping; smoking was decreasing as vaping was increasing, which debunked the talking point that vaping was a gateway to smoking; etc.), but it's not surprising that none of this mattered. After all, once The Kids are thrown out as the reason for legislation, any opposition to it gets spun as opposition against *kids*, which, you don't have to be a polling expert to know, doesn't exactly go over well. You also don't have to be a market expert to know that, in the wake of the ban, other products simply filled the hole that had been left by the banning of fruit-flavored pods: fruit-flavored disposables.

My commitment to small government has placed me in the line of "Think of the Children!" fire more times than I can count. It happens often regarding my views on legalizing all drugs, despite the fact that these views are actually *not* based on the fact that I don't care if kids overdose and die.

They're based on a few other things, such as the fact that the War on Drugs has been an objective failure, and "objective" is no exaggeration. Just a few examples: After laws cracking down on doctors writing opiate prescriptions caused opiate prescriptions to fall, opiate-related fatalities actually went up, likely due to people turning to the black market instead. Meanwhile, chronic pain patients struggled to get the medication they needed to live normal lives, and the increased restrictions were associated with increased risks of suicide and death for those patients. We spent about $9 billion going after opium and heroin production in Afghanistan only for Afghan farmers to be growing poppies on four times as much land in 2018 as they had been growing it in 2002, and for a lot of the suspected drug labs we did go after to turn out to be empty mud structures.

People do sometimes try to dunk on me by pointing out the failures of drug decriminalization in places like Portland, but they fail to understand that "decriminalization" and "legalization" are two different things—with the former, all of the issues that come with prohibition and the ability to obtain certain drugs only on the black market will still apply.

There's also the fact that we can't say we live in a free society if we are literally locking people up for deciding what to put into their own bodies. I could go on forever, but the point of this book is not necessarily to get you to agree with me, but to get you to understand that I have concrete, research-based reasons for my beliefs, regardless of attacks from people like LittleDog4 on Twitter/X: **You think all drugs should be legal? Does that include the ones killing kids? You're a real disappointment.**

Like—what? I mean, so, so, so many questions. What drugs are "the ones killing kids"? Are there some drugs out there that specifically kill kids *and only kids* if kids touch them? Plus, there is absolutely such a thing as kids dying from taking too much of an over-the-counter medication such as a cold medicine or cough syrup—should those be illegal?

Let's give her some credit and say she does mean opioids. I mean, some of the statistics *are* harrowing. Like how opioids were responsible for a whopping 52.2 percent of child deaths in 2018, a huge increase from the 24.1 percent in 2005.

It's a tragic situation, but that doesn't mean that the War on Drugs is the best way to solve it. For one thing, increasing overdose deaths among teens doesn't necessarily mean increased drug use. In fact, as an April 2022 NPR piece points out, a JAMA network study from the same month found that drug use among teens ages fourteen to eighteen decreased during the pandemic, but overdose deaths increased anyway, with 77 percent of them involving fentanyl in 2021.

For another, experts often explain that teens aren't seeking out fentanyl, or even heroin, on purpose. Dr. Nora Volkow, director of the National Institute on Drug Abuse, told NPR, "Teenagers don't seek out illicit opioids, [but] they do seek out prescription opioids and that has always been one of their favorite drugs: Vicodin, OxyContin, hydrocodone." She adds, "They also seek out benzodiazepines."

The problem, she says, is that the teenagers often unknowingly buy fake versions of these pills . . . ones that look like the real thing, but are actually "illicitly manufactured" and "contaminated with fentanyl." Although NPR notes that Volkow wasn't involved in the JAMA study, its authors reached similar conclusions: "Since 2015, fentanyls have been increasingly added to counterfeit pills resembling prescription opioids, benzodiazepines, and other drugs, which adolescents may not identify as dangerous and which may be playing a key role in these shifts."

The statistics here agree with me, but even if you don't, and even if your reason is moral-emotional, that's fine. But you have to at least admit that I think these things for some reason, and that the reason can't actually be that I just don't care when kids die. (For what it's worth, I have loved people who have died due to drugs; including someone I was *in love* with. It's something I thought about including in this book, but ultimately decided to save for another one.) Again: Absolutely everyone, with the very rare exception of the truly sick and twisted person, does care when kids die, and deep down, everyone understands that. Including you, or else you wouldn't have been so taken aback by the way I started this chapter! Now, reminding yourself of this does mean you'll have to acknowledge that the disagreement you're having is a difference of opinion over policy, and not a difference of opinion over the importance of kids' safety, forcing you to take yourself down a peg, which can be difficult, especially during the heat of an argument. Ironically, though, it's also going to be the only way you'll have hope of bringing the heat down enough to have a productive conversation.

Anyway, although it's usually the Right employing the "Think of the Children!" argument when it comes to drugs, the Left sure does employ this argument, too—often, about weapons.

For instance, Democratic Connecticut Sen. Chris Murphy, who said in a *Salon* interview: "It is beyond me why Republicans who claim to care about the health of our kids don't seem to give a crap about our children who are being exposed to these epidemic, cataclysmic rates of gun violence."

Like, bro. It's simply not true that Republicans just don't "give a crap" about kids being victims of gun violence. If anything, offering such an outlandish explanation is the last way anyone who wants to solve an issue should go about doing so. If you want to be constructive, the first thing you should do here is try to understand why it *really* is that people oppose gun control. For many people, myself included, there's argument enough in the fact that it's our Second Amendment right. Put another way? It's *not* that people aren't concerned about their kids being shot, it's that they *are* concerned about their kids growing up in a country where they would have less protection against government tyranny. President Biden tried to mock those of us with this fear in a speech in June 2021, saying: "If you think you need to have weapons to take on the government, you need F-15s and maybe some nuclear weapons," but to me? All it takes to see the ridiculousness of that is to realize that that "logic" would technically apply to our rights under all Amendments. Like, "Oh, you think you need a right to free speech to stand up to the government? Well, we could just nuke your asses!" Plus, not to give the U.S. government too much credit, but I do think our leaders at least realize that the downsides to nuking the shit out of their own people would make it a not-so-great option for them to go that far. For them to do so would *not* be reasonable; so, in an even remotely reasonable world, guns are a reasonable deterrent.

It would be better for us as a society to acknowledge people's real reasons for their views rather than tearing people apart unnecessarily by lobbing insane accusations, like them not caring about kids dying.

Of course, politicians are the least likely to do this, for the reason I repeat throughout this book: They gain power over demonization. People will be far more motivated to vote for them if they think that the Other Side doesn't care if their children die, so I see why they do it. It's an easy way for them to score political points!

They do the same thing with immigration. The Left screams about kids in cages, which gets them points. The Right screams about kids dying at the hands of coyotes, which gets *them* points. What it doesn't prompt them to do is their job, which is to solve our clearly broken immigration system.

Whatever you think the answer is here, you should still take notice of how much more interested our politicians seem in pontificating about these problems than actually solving them. Remember the DREAMers? Flashback, right? Well, it's up to Congress to give them real protection under the law (as opposed to flimsy executive-power protection that can be taken away), but they haven't. Sure, many of them screamed about the importance of such protection during the Trump administration, but none of them moved to solidify it once Trump was out. It seems pretty clear, to me, that they don't actually care about solving the problem as much as they aim to portray that they do when they're exploiting it for political gain. After all, people who do care about fixing something tend to at least try, especially when they have the power to do so. But if your aim is exploitation, solving the problem is not just unnecessary but potentially detrimental, because it could limit your opportunities to exploit it for political benefit in the future.

Pivoting the subject a little, the government often uses "Think of the Children!" not only to garner political points but also to push rights-grabbing legislation—and some of it is far more consequential than the right to bear Mango Juul pods that I discussed earlier in this chapter.

In the summer of 2023, Republican Sen. Lindsay Graham and Democratic Sen. Elizabeth Warren aimed to convince us that we desperately needed their legislation to shut down Section 230, "writing" (I don't think these politicians actually write their stuff themselves, do they?) in a *New York Times* op-ed: "Giant digital platforms have provided new avenues of proliferation for the sexual abuse and exploitation of children, human trafficking, drug trafficking and bullying and have promoted eating disorders, addictive behaviors and teen suicide."

They were far from the first to frame it this way. In March 2023, Democratic Sen. Dick Durbin shared during a Senate Judiciary Subcommittee that one of the witnesses from a Judiciary Committee meeting a few weeks earlier was "a mother with a son who died by suicide after he was mercilessly bullied on anonymous messaging apps," adding that "[t]here were several other mothers in attendance carrying color photos of their kids who suffered similar heartbreak."

"In addition to tragically losing children, these mothers had something else in common: they couldn't hold the online platforms that played a role in their child's death accountable," he said. "The reason? Section 230."

Now, I'll explain what Section 230 is in a second; I got you. But you don't have to know what Section 230 to see what they did there: The way they set that debate, if you *don't* support legislation limiting it—and instead see Section 230 as being good—then you must not care if kids in this country become trafficked anorexics. That is if they don't kill themselves first.

But Section 230 *is* good. The passionate bipartisan disdain for it makes this statement controversial, which is why I felt like I must be some kind of masochist on my way home from doing my guest-host monologue for *Gutfeld!* on the topic in February 2023.

But I'm glad I did. For one thing? There are real concerns when it comes to free speech if this law were compromised, and it feels great to know that I stuck to my principles. For another? It's going to save me literal *minutes* of writing time for this chapter, because I can just copy and paste what I said then to explain what I mean:

> [Section 230 is] a short law written in 1996 that's said to have created the internet, and goes like this:
>
> "No provider or user of an interactive computer service shall be treated as the publisher or speaker of any information provided by another information content provider."
>
> Those words allowed the internet to grow exponentially over the past 25 years because sites like Google, Twitter, YouTube and Facebook couldn't be sued over the content users post on their platforms.
>
> [. . .]
>
> But recently, both political sides have argued in favor of ending Section 230.
>
> For liberals, it's about the "hate speech" on the platform.

Of course, their definition of hate speech is broader than a Kardashian's ass.

For conservatives, it's about wanting to hold big tech liable for silencing or shadowbanning their views.

Like crazy conspiracy theories about gross stuff on Hunter Biden's laptop.

Which could be traced back to . . . gross stuff on Hunter Biden's laptop.

But all of the bad things about big tech—and a desire for your voice to be heard—are exactly why you should want to keep Section 230.

If you think that big tech censorship is bad now, just imagine how many more things would get censored if these platforms had to worry about getting sued.

It would be like trying to watch the movie *Scarface* as if it was edited by Dana Perino. It would be 10 minutes long and about dogs.

Bottom line: These platforms would be most worried about getting sued by those with the greatest means to do so—the powerful.

And if companies like Twitter have to worry about that, and they know that it's basically impossible to keep track of everything being posted—don't you think that they might just automatically decide to ban any mention of those people at all?

[. . .]

So without Section 230, I'm afraid that the ability to speak truth to power on the internet might completely disappear.

No civilian should want to see the destruction of our ability to speak truth to power on the internet. But frame it as "Law That Makes

Kids Kill Themselves While Heartless Tech Companies Get Rich off of the Literal Blood of Children, Those Bastards," and it makes it a lot less likely you'll want to even think about opposing it. But that doesn't make the facts any less true.

Section 230, of course, is also far from the only time The Kids have been invoked as a catalyst for more restrictive technology laws. In the spring of 2023, the government pushed the RESTRICT Act, known colloquially in the media as a bill to ban TikTok.

Congresswoman Mary Miller (R-IL) spoke out in favor of the ban, saying, "The Chinese Communist Party should not be allowed to conduct psychological warfare on our children." Sen. John Thune (R-SD) said:

> The threat to kids these days—there is a very dark side to social
> media and to the digital age, and I think we have to be vigilant
> about that. It's not only young boys, it's young girls—we've
> heard lots of testimony with respect to Instagram in particular
> and the impact that it has on teens and preteens, just a lot of
> social problems created with this . . . and I think that what we
> address here, of course, is the national security implication, but
> I think as a general matter, we need more accountability and
> we need more transparency from the social media platforms . . .
> these algorithms that kick in, they keep feeding people, they get
> into bubbles, and in many cases it's a lot of stuff that I certainly
> know parents would not want their kids exposed to.

Democratic Sen. Dan Sullivan said that TikTok had a "troubling influence over our children." Democratic Sen. Richard Blumenthal called TikTok "a clear and present danger to both national security and children's safety."

Republican Rep. Michael McCaul of Texas bragged that "both

sides of the aisle were standing together saying this is a threat to our children, and we need to stop it."

Basically, if you failed to support this bill, you were not only an anti-American, China-humping traitor, but you were also an anti-American, China-humping traitor who did not care if an entire generation of children grew up to be anti-American, China-humping traitors just like you and your unpatriotic, idiotic, China-humping ass.

How on Earth could anyone argue against that? You couldn't! Well, except for maybe by actually reading the bill, which is exactly what I did to prepare to co-host *The Big Saturday Show*, giving me the chance to offer an unpopular but important warning about the RESTRICT Act, something I was admittedly nervous about doing effectively, especially given that the segment had clearly been framed as one to mock Rep. Alexandria Ocasio-Cortez for coming out against the legislation.

I explained that the bill didn't simply say "this bans TikTok," but would give "broad, general, vague powers to the government" to determine whether "a certain app or a technology company is 'a threat to national security,' and it could be interpreted by the government however it wants."

"I just look at the past, and the way that things have gotten through because of 'a threat to national security'—something like the Patriot Act, which is purportedly because of 'terrorism' and 'we need it to keep us safe and this and that,' is being used other ways and . . . abused," I said, adding: "So, I'm just not at a point in my life where I'm able to say, 'You know what, government? I think that you *should* have this new, vague power, and I trust you to use it in this way, that's only to protect us from foreign adversaries.' Because the government can also be an adversary against us when it has powers that are abused. I oppose tyranny in all of its forms, including from our own United States government."

After I made this comment, other panelists admitted to me that I'd made them think of the issue differently, and that they hadn't even read the bill. Thankfully, in the following week or so, other Fox News hosts would come out against the bill as well, and it would eventually wind up paused.

Unfortunately, in April 2024, Biden signed the so-called (and *very* vague) "Protecting Americans from Foreign Adversary Controlled Applications Act," which would ban TikTok unless the app's Chinese parent company, ByteDance, sells it to an American buyer before the January 19, 2025, deadline.

As I explained on *Gutfeld!* at the time, however, this bill has many of the same issues as the previously proposed legislation. To me, it would clearly violate the First Amendment rights to free expression of the Americans who use the app, as well as the Fifth Amendment rights—which require the government to convict you of a crime before taking your property—of the Americans who have ownership in it. Sen. Rand Paul pointed all of this out in an April 2024 piece for *Reason*. As another *Reason* piece, this one by Elizabeth Nolan Brown, points out, the possible Fifth Amendment concerns are "an important—and often overlooked—factor in all of this: No one has produced evidence of any specific legal infractions committed by TikTok, let alone proven such offenses took place." Now, I'm not saying that there aren't any reasons to believe that TikTok is a tool of the Chinese Communist Party. There are, but such a belief, no matter how well-founded, is still very different from actually proving it from a legal standpoint.

What's more, like the other bill, this one also does not limit the scope of its power to TikTok specifically. Far from it: Its vague language, and particularly its broad definition of what constitutes a "foreign adversary controlled application," opens the door for the government to control, or even outright ban, a wide range of companies, especially given the broad discretion it also gives to the president to decide where it does and does not apply.

At the time of publication, the future of this legislation (and the many possible legal challenges to it) remains to be seen.

In any case, anytime you hear the government use words such as "security" and "safety," you absolutely *should* be vigilant . . . about how the government might be using that kind of language to manipulate you. Often, it aims to get you on board with giving up your own rights (à la the Patriot Act) or to throw your support behind another war built on lies (see my "Half-Veteran" chapter). Other times, people with an agenda use words like "safe" and "safety" to divide us.

Republicans might suggest that children aren't safe from "woke" teaching (or even straight-up grooming) in schools, and Democrats might say that children aren't safe from transphobia in schools. Ultimately, they can use fearmongering to convince you to support legislation that threatens your rights, specific examples of which I'll discuss more in my chapters about gender. After all, when the Other Side is a just group with which you may disagree, that's one thing. But when the Other Side threatens your very safety and/or the well-being of innocent children? That's a different story, and you'll think less about what powers you're giving the government when a politician proposes a way to fix what they've made you fear.

As I said earlier: Whenever I hear language from the government that's clearly meant to evoke fear, I ask myself two questions: Who or what does the government want me to be afraid of? And what do they gain if they succeed?

Now, I want to acknowledge something: It *is* easier to *not* speak out negatively once The Kids have entered the conversation. And in many cases—such as a friend asking you how cute her clearly ugly baby is—it isn't worth it to push back. When it comes to political debates, however, it often is, not only because of what we can lose in terms of our rights but also what we can lose in terms of our relationships.

Think about it: Although government and media can use fear to divide us for their own gain, we as human beings can use it to unite us.

I was once in a Fox News greenroom listening to a very famous

Republican talking head speaking with a very famous Democratic talking head about how terrifying it is for them to have children in school amid so many shootings. The Democrat explained she felt safer because she lived in a liberal area where people didn't really own guns, while the Republican said she had pulled her daughter out of public school over her fears, opting instead for a private school that had extra security measures.

And guess what? Neither tried to argue with the other about the approach she had taken in response to her fear. What's more? They seemed to bond over the shared fear, despite being two women who most certainly routinely get shit on for not Thinking of the Children by different sides for different reasons.

It's something I talk about over and over again in this book, and the reason I do that is not because I am running out of things to say (I could never, although I'm sure there have been people in my life who have prayed for it) but because it is important: Too often, people scream at each other over having opposite or different solutions, while missing the chance to acknowledge that they care about the same problem. Debate is healthy and wonderful, but our humanity should, at the very least, lead us to acknowledge this—if not explicitly, then at least in terms of how we approach the other person. Rather than accuse someone of being a pedophile or a sociopath, realize that having a different opinion about the best way to solve a problem without introducing prohibitively negative externalities is not the same as believing that the problem doesn't matter.

9

Drag Queens Saved My Life

When I was in the middle of what I would eventually learn would be, I don't know, my sixty-seventh? and final breakup from my abusive Nightmare of a Boyfriend, drag queens taught me something that would help me in getting through it for good.

I'm being serious! Therapy was a huge part, yes, but I don't want to discount the role of the drag queens.

Here's what happened: Toward the end of the relationship, Nightmare was "touring" for comedy (a lot of that was just doing open mics and bar shows in different locations), and I traveled to watch his shows in Detroit. I flew myself there, took him to all my favorite restaurants, and tried not to let him see me freaking out about my family finding out that I'd gone to Detroit without telling them. The way I'd explained it to him, I just didn't want to stress about the time and logistics of seeing everyone while I was there.

The truth? During one of our many breakups, I'd admitted to my pal Meghan McCain, who then alerted my dad and Kennedy, that I actually *hadn't* been hit by a Seamless guy on a bike a few months prior when I'd shown up to work covered in bruises with my arm in a sling. What had actually happened? Depends on who you ask! The way he explained it, *I* had been physically abusive in grabbing on to *him* at the door and beg-

ging him not to go, terrified that he might do that thing again where he
ghosted me for weeks or longer because I somehow believed I was nothing without him. At the time, I actually believed it was my fault, even
after I saw my body absolutely covered in bruises, even after the pain got
so bad I wound up needing to go to the emergency room for my injuries, even though this wasn't the only time things had gotten physical,
even after my therapist had made me explain out loud that he—a man
more than a foot taller than I was and more than double my weight—
clearly could have handled the situation in a way that didn't result in
injuries so bad the hospital actually gave me an opiate prescription in
2017, the height of the opiate-prescriptions crackdown. When he very
begrudgingly came to the hospital, he sat there liking Instagram photos
of other girls he had been lying to me about having slept with while we
were seeing each other and accused me of only being there for attention,
adding, "The nurses were visibly upset with you." I bought all of it; I
felt *so* bad for putting us in this situation. So much so that I remember
sending him sexy photos of myself *with my arm in the sling*. Jesus, Kat.
Just . . . *dear God*. Anyway, I went back to New York City alone after
the Detroit leg of his "tour." I had to get back to work, and he had a few
more shows to do in the Midwest. While he was still out of town, and
being less than communicative with me, I'd make the "mistake" of calling him to express some of my insecurities about our relationship—you
know, stuff like how it bothered me that he would not let me over his
apartment ever when his roommates were home because (and he *admitted* this) he did not want them to know we were together—leading him
to go completely nuts on me about how I never cared about him or his
feelings, and I was absolutely exhausting him by taking so much from
him emotionally and never giving anything back.

After this fight, I'd message him on Facebook, telling him I wanted
to talk, that I couldn't stand the silence. I said that since we were in a
relationship we should talk through these things, pleading for him to at

least let me know when we could talk again, and then saying, **I'm literally just wanting to know if I am in a relationship or not**, to which he replied: **Message me one more fucking time and we won't be.**

He finally reached out. Four days later. With a simple **How are you?** And so we made plans to go to dinner when he got back in a few days like nothing happened. I mean, I'd just gone through days of absolute hell for bringing up my issues with the relationship; I wasn't going to make the mistake of doing that again. But I'll tell you more about those four days in a bit. First, I want to let you know that, just a day or two after we made those dinner plans, and just hours before we were supposed to honor them, we would instead break up over Facebook Messenger—to the absolute delight of my friends. Thinking back, the shift in the tone of the conversation between us happened after I mentioned that, after about a year or so of not doing stand-up, I was going to do a set at the Comedy Cellar's Village Underground (one of the hardest clubs, if not *the* hardest club, to get booked at): **Just to 'try stand-up again,' you get booked at the Cellar, while [y]ou just watch me bust my fucking ass in the shittiest parts of the country**, he'd said, referring to his aforementioned "tour."

Looking back, I should have expected that reaction. I'd seen him rage over my success before, like the time he angrily jumped out of a romantic bath and stormed home after I told him I'd gotten a raise during a month that he'd ghosted me, or the time he randomly flew into a rage and started screaming at me to "go fuck [my] rich neighbors," again storming out. Often, out of nowhere, he would blame me for his career not going anywhere, saying how messed up it was that I didn't do more to help him. I had made some introductions for him, but he kept bombing those opportunities. What I should have said was: "I did all I could; I can't make you *good*, bro." But I didn't! Instead, my focus was avoiding his anger because I just couldn't take it, even though I knew logically that this "relationship" would never work out, and that I honestly didn't even want it to. I guess it was that he'd done such a good job of convincing me that I was so terrible, I could never hope to have any other relationship, let alone one that was any better.

But according to that angry Facebook conversation, the real nut of it for Nightmare was that I was a selfish, horrible person . . . who was apparently also a meth addict? As I've never done meth even once (not to brag), I believe he was referring to my Vyvanse, which I take as prescribed for my ADHD.

Anyway, back to the four days between the original fight and the "How are you?" that led us to making those dinner plans that we wouldn't keep. His silent treatment affected me the way it always did, which was that it decimated me. This "relationship" was, if you couldn't tell, an extremely abusive, trauma-bonded situation, something Dr. Drew would later explain to me as a Cult of Two, where reality made no difference, making it difficult for me to eat, fall asleep without Benadryl, or get out of bed once I had managed to pass out. Getting out of bed, after all, meant having to look at my phone and deal with the horrific realization that he hadn't texted me.

Here's where the drag queens come in.

In the middle of those four days, I managed to pull myself out of bed to meet a friend at a drag show at the legendary Pieces in the West Village, and I was struck by the confidence and irreverence the drag queens displayed. Not only were they unapologetically themselves, but they also looked amazing doing it. What a contrast to how I was living: Apologizing for things I hadn't done. Apologizing for the things *he* had done because I had "pushed" him to do them. Apologizing for how my success had made him feel. Hiding anything and everything about myself that I thought might make him uncomfortable. I was a complete slave to the sensibilities of another human being, and a drab one at that, while these queens were glammed up being whoever the fuck they wanted to be.

It was intoxicating. So much so that when they asked for audience volunteers for a dance-off, I shot my hand up in the air so enthusiastically I was chosen, even though I a.) lacked a penis and b.) was wearing far less makeup than anyone there. When it was my turn, I flailed around, twerked like an inflatable tube man at a car dealership in the middle of a tornado, kicked my legs in the air—and the whole place was cheering. I'm not a good dancer, but I do know how to get a room going. Or maybe it was how bad I was that made it a worthwhile spectacle, kind of like the World's Ugliest Dog competition. In any case, I had the room going far, far more than any other dancer, and wound up tying for first. (They couldn't give me *First*-First, I assume, because of the aforementioned lack of a penis.)

I carried the energy with me all the way home and into the next day, and even texted my therapist about it. He replied with something along the lines of: "See what you're able to accomplish without him? See what kind of happiness you're able to have without him? See how you're able to *be yourself* without him?" I carried it into that set I did at the Village Underground, and even dared to joke about what a dumpster fire the "relationship" was onstage:

Who here is in a relationship? Anyone here who doesn't know if they're in a relationship or not? Cool, cool. Just me then, I guess. I'm not worried about North Korea; do you know why? Because I think that Kim Jong Un is having far too much fun fighting with Trump to let him go. I have been in so many relationships like that. I might be in one right now but I'm not sure because we got into a fight and haven't spoken in three days. That's not a joke, that's just a little bit about Kat.

As the months dragged on and it became clear that the breakup was for real this time, and I was just a walking open wound, a shell of a person trying to get on my feet and remember who I was, I routinely looked back on my night at Pieces with the queens and channeled them in an attempt to give me a glimmer of hope in that darkness. Maybe, just maybe, I could be as fierce and confident and self-loving.

I really admire and relate to drag queens, even beyond our shared getting-ready-for-work routines of fake hair, chest padding, fake lashes, and enough makeup to be concerned that I couldn't hug anyone without leaving a Shroud of Turin–esque imprint of my face on their clothing. Drag queens are a sort of living embodiment of the subjects I discussed in my first book: Everything can be mocked, nothing is sacred, and self-expression is the key not only to personal happiness but also to connection with those around us. We have a lot of the same attitudes on decorum (basically, that it's overrated and it's important to fly in the face of it) and every time I see one, I can't help but feel like we would probably really get along. Well, I suppose in some cases, at least until they somehow found out that I work at Fox News.

I love drag queens, and I'll never pretend otherwise, not even when someone hates me for loving them, which, of course, has happened. I think my all-time favorite expression of this hate was when some guy called for my firing because I said that I, a thirtysomething adult, enjoy watching *RuPaul's Drag Race*.

Here's the exact wording, because *obviously* I screenshot and saved this gem: **Kat loves watching the drag queen show she just said. Gutfeld get her wacko lib annoying personality off the show. I know you're loyal but she ruins the show. Can't watch anymore.** Second place: **I'll bet your husband is ashamed of you for what you have said lately about drag. Nuf said.** And third place: **With drag queens we let it be fun to long It's wrong period.** (I kept the original errors, just to make sure you had the full picture.) The thing is, I've always openly celebrated drag queens on Fox News, to the point that I once even appointed myself "probably the most pro–drag queen person on any network."

My love for drag even once prompted me to do something I very rarely do: I interrupted Tyrus during an episode of *Gutfeld!* because he said drag was just "lip-syncing," which "is not a talent."

"I want you to try and walk around in heels," I said.

"Why would I want to, I'm a grown-ass—"

"Because you can't do it!" I shouted. "It's very difficult."

It's absurd to say drag doesn't require any talent when you couldn't even manage the walk to the stage. You don't have to like it, but considering drag anything short of art is inaccurate. It requires not just walking, but *dancing* in heels. It also demands that you have enough imagination to create and develop a unique character, complete with costuming—I mean, *serious* costuming, the wardrobe and makeup you'll see in drag shows often rivals what you'll see on Broadway—and choreography. It requires charisma to work the crowd. It doesn't have to be your kind of art, but saying it's not art is just wrong, and if you think it's gross and have no interest in watching it, then that's your right, but *just say that.* You can't claim to be an authoritative voice on a subject you don't know enough about. It's the exact reason why I would never claim to know what makes a good running back. Why? Because I don't know what a running back is, and I even had to Google it to see if it was two words or one.

In general, whenever drag-related outrage has been the subject of a segment, I've elected to view it as a story about anything or anyone else because, well, drag queens are people. I would know . . . many of my friends have performed drag. The flower girl at my wedding was a thirty-two-year-old man in heels, a tutu, and a flower crown, who added a smoky eye and strip lashes for his after-party look.

Of course, a lot of the outrage these days is often presented as a fight against the sexualization of children. Before I go any further, because things have gotten so nuts that I actually need to say this: Sexualizing children is bad and weird.

Still? It's just not true that the mere existence of drag or gay relationships, even in public, amounts to grooming or sexually abusing kids.

I spent my last chapter talking about how "Think of the Children!" can radicalize and polarize people, whipping them into a fear-driven frenzy that leaves no room to stop and consider the implications of legislation. As promised, I'll give a few examples of how that's been happening regarding issues specifically related to sex and gender, but first, I want to talk about something else that knee-jerk outrage can keep us from missing: opportunities for creativity.

Let me explain: Earlier in this book, I talked about how binary thinking is the enemy of critical thinking. Once you pick a side, you don't need to think critically; you just go along with whatever your side is saying. Outrage only compounds the problem, as critical thinking is always less likely when you're blinded by strong emotions. I've said it before, but I'll say it again: Although it's certainly true that "Facts don't care about your feelings," it's also true that feelings don't care about your facts. They are by definition irrational, and having moments when we're emotional rather than rational is all part of the human experience. It's definitely the only explanation for why I even dated a loser like Nightmare in the first place!

Here, I want to mention that binary thinking and the knee-jerk outrage it creates can make us miss thinking not only critically, but also creatively. I've noticed that the freedom from predetermined narratives and manufactured outrage has allowed me to think of jokes I might otherwise have missed.

During Pride Month in 2023, North Face featured a drag queen in one of its ads, inviting people to "come out . . . in nature" and "to celebrate Pride and bring camp to the outdoors." The reaction to the ad was mostly divided into two sides, with the Right being outraged at North Face for going "woke," and the Left being outraged at the Right for being outraged.

When I had the chance to give my take on the ad on *Gutfeld!*, however, I simply quipped that it was an unrealistic commercial because drag queens don't camp, but lesbians sure do. If they wanted to do a Pride-themed commercial, why would they not feature a lesbian instead?

Or there was the time we were doing a segment about a hot, curvy mom who wore the same skintight leotard that a drag performer had worn during an after-school performance at a *high school*. (The italics are meant to indicate my confusion that this was even a controversy in the first place. Lady, high school kids have already seen the "scandalous" sight of a man in a leotard if they have access to the internet . . . and/ or a performance of Disney On Ice.) The mom wore the outfit in some show of "See? This isn't appropriate for me to wear at this meeting! How is it appropriate to wear in front of The Kids!" Uh, because it was a drag performance, lady. Disney On Ice costumes wouldn't be "appropriate" for meetings, either, but that doesn't make them salacious.

Here, seeing beyond the "Brave Hot Mom Stands Up Against Woke in Schools!" framing of the segment gave me a great opening for a self-deprecating joke: "I also need to wear fake hair, fake lashes, and a big padded bra to look noticeably female, so I have a lot in common with [drag queens]. If I was that mom and I tried to wear that outfit and I went there, they'd be like, 'It's a drag queen again!'" (Note: The mom turned out to be less than a hero. While looking her up as part of my research for this book, I learned that she'd later end up pleading guilty to falsely accusing one of her business partner's kids of sexually abusing their sibling. Woof.)

Anyway! For some of the people watching me in these segments, my own lack of outrage was enough to make me a target of theirs—earning me the sorts of rageful comments I've come to expect ever since drag queens became controversial. I say "became" here on purpose, because it certainly hasn't always been this way. My outspoken love of drag queens wasn't new. It didn't start when drag queens became a major part of the news cycle, circa 2022 or 2023; what *was* new was people berating me over it. I realized this when I was looking through old clips for this chapter and found one from September 2021, when I commented that I would never watch *The Crown* unless a drag queen was playing Queen Elizabeth.

Did I have people calling for my firing? Were they enraged that I was supporting groomers? Or that I was erasing women by calling for a man in "woman face" to take a role belonging to a biological woman?

No. No one said any of that. No one said anything at all. I know this for a fact because I even searched tweets mentioning me with the words "drag" or "crown" from around that time, and all that I was able to find was one single tweet telling me that I should consider watching *The Crown* anyway.

What happened between now and then? What always seems to happen: Politics and polarization entered the chat, making us suddenly hate each other over something we hadn't thought to hate each other for before, with each side driving harder and harder on their own points beyond all reason or rationality, intent on proving that they are not part of that Evil Other.

Going forward, I'm going to talk about Drag Stuff and Trans/Gender Stuff under the same umbrella, because that's how they've been presented all too often in media, even though their pairing has become a bit of a hilarious display of lack of actual knowledge or consideration of reality.

This has perhaps never been clearer than during a *Gutfeld!* segment about a one-piece bathing suit modeled by a man in which everyone assumed that the male model *must* be trans or nonbinary simply because of the women's-style bathing suit choice.

Newsflash: Wearing women's-style clothing doesn't make you trans. Men who identify as men wear women's clothes sometimes. Many of these men enjoy sex with other men, others are just, like, in post-punk revival bands or whatever.

Speaking of "they/them," choosing to use people's preferred pronouns has also somehow become evidence that you're part of an Evil Other for far too many people in my Twitter/X mentions. I know I've already stated that I'm a free speech absolutist, and that I wrote a book about my commitment to free speech, but just in case I need to say this anyway: Although I choose to use people's preferred pronouns, I vehemently oppose the idea of any law that would make using this language mandatory.

Yep! Contrary to the unhinged allegations often lobbed my way from many on the Right, my choice to use whatever pronoun a person requests actually does *not* mean that I support speech laws, or that I'm a groomer, or even a liberal. For me, it just comes down to: This world can be a sad, lonely, scary place. We're all stressed about a million different things all the time, and every one of them is nothing more than our own conditioning distracting us from what we should really be stressed out about, which is that every moment that goes by brings us another moment closer to our certain death. (Honestly? I have never been able to understand the popularity of the saying: "It will be okay in the end! If it's not okay, it's not the end." Like, the end is the worst part, actually? You die?)

In many ways, life is nothing more than a hospital waiting room. The stuff like sex and anger and finding a parking spot is just life's version of the room's germ-covered magazines, meant to keep our mind off of our mortality and pass the time. All of this to say: If you happen to be someone whose own emotional torment can be eased even slightly by, say, simply having others refer to you as "they" instead of "she," then yeah, I'm absolutely going to give that to you. Oh, and there's also the fact that using "they" to refer to a single, unspecified person is something that many of us already do; I do it throughout this book to avoid the clunkiness of "he or she." Some people may do it without even realizing that they're doing it. For example: "I hate when someone says they use 'they/them' pronouns!"

My view's the same when it comes to any adult choosing to live the one short life they've been given as a trans person. I mean damn, I have enough trouble making my own life decisions, why would I ever think I'm qualified to insert myself into someone else's? When you break it down, it's just an individual making a choice that makes them happy that hurts no one else . . . to me, there's nothing objectionable or even slightly scandalous about that. If you're happy, then I'm happy for you. Of course, where the argument over these issues often gets stuck is: One group in mass confusion over what it even *means* to be nonbinary or trans, with those people saying they simply don't and can't understand it, or that they think it's made up. The other group is those who do identify as trans or nonbinary (and the activists who support them), who respond by digging their heels in about how being trans or nonbinary is valid and real and actually *so* easy to understand.

What you get are two sides just shouting at and over each other about something that neither side is going to change their mind about, when really, they could just agree to disagree and respect each other anyway. To me, whether you subscribe to it, or even understand it, shouldn't be a determining factor. You don't have to subscribe to anything to do something that costs you nothing to make another person happy. (Again: I do believe that this should be a choice, and that no one should ever be forced to use certain language, and if you want more of my thoughts on language, read the book I wrote about it.)

Doing something that costs me nothing to make another person happy is my go-to when it comes to a lot more than just preferred pronouns. I am not religious (unfortunately, because I think I'd be happier if I were), but if I'm ever having dinner at someone's house, and they all bow their heads in prayer before a meal, I don't think twice before doing the exact same thing. If I am at a Catholic Mass for a wedding, I stand when I'm supposed to stand, and I sit when I'm supposed to sit. I do this despite the fact that I'm not only not Catholic anymore but have also experienced a lot of difficulty in some of my family relationships for having lapsed.

You don't have to understand the depths of a person's beliefs to respect them. I mean, I guess except for whoever might say: "I will never use anyone's preferred pronouns, because there have been examples of children who were harmed by transitioning too early or were confused about their identity by someone in the movement, so therefore, the whole thing is bad." Because obviously, there are, you know, *zero* examples of anyone in the Church ever harming or traumatizing a child. You get my sarcasm-drenched point, as I'm far from the first person to have used it. The difference in the way I am using it from the way I have seen others using it, though, is that I don't intend it to prove Trans and Drag Good, Church and Christians Bad, so much as to share my encompassing view that no bad individual or act that occurred within a sect of theology or philosophy should be used to color every one of its members.

Some of the same people who spent years criticizing Democrats for demonizing all Republicans as Nazis—and rightly so!—don't seem to see the irony of basically doing the same thing by insisting that all Democrats are pedophiles. (It goes without saying, of course, that it isn't true. Being gay, or lesbian, or a Democrat, or a drag queen does not mean that you are a pedophile. Molesting children means that you're a pedophile. Got it?)

But the "NO SEX STUFF AROUND KIDS PERIOD, YOU PEDO-PHILE!" shouting has become so loud that not even the clearest of logic seems to have the ability to cut through it. If that wasn't obvious to you already, consider that in March 2023, a principal at Tallahassee Classical School, a public charter school aiming to provide "a content-rich classical education," "resigned" after apparently running afoul of the New Pedophilia Rules. I put "resigned" in quotes because it was hardly really a resignation; she had been given the choice between resigning and being fired. She admitted that she'd had a few other issues at the school, but the demand for her resignation came after this one.

And what was this nail-in-the-coffin issue, exactly?

She allowed a teacher to include a photo of Michelangelo's *David* in a sixth-grade art history lesson without warning the students' parents beforehand, and three parents complained.

Why?

Because the statue has a penis, making it inappropriate for their twelve-year-olds and even downright "pornographic," according to one of the parents. "It," again, being one of the most famous pieces of art in the history of the world.

When I went on my honeymoon to Florence with Cam, we made it a point to see *David* because we had heard it was just breathtaking to see in person. And it was. It was almost hard to comprehend how there wouldn't have been something supernatural involved in its creation. And guess what? When I say all of that, I'm not talking about his dick. What's more, neither were the friends who had recommended it to me. As large and diverse as the crowd surrounding the statue was, there wasn't even a single person jerking off. It's not porn. Seriously, put up a video of the statue of *David* on PornHub and see how many clicks it gets.

It's never occurred to me or any other sane person to look at such a beautiful, iconic piece of art and think of it as sexual. I didn't bring sex into it, parents in Tallahassee did, and with such fervor that someone got *fired*.

The chairman of the school board, Barney Bishop II, defended the decision this way: "[The principal] wasn't let go because of the artistic nude pictures. We show it every year to our students. The problem with this issue was the lack of follow-through on the process," meaning that parents weren't notified ahead of time.

Now, you can absolutely argue in favor of parents having control over what the schools are teaching their kids. I would know; I so often argue exactly this. But this doesn't mean that insane stuff like this story isn't worthy of examination. In addition to being insane, it also represents a deviation from the past. I mean, Michelangelo's *David* has probably been taught in schools for literal centuries by now, and this is the first time I've heard anyone earnestly call it "pornographic," let alone for such accusations to play a huge role in a person's firing.

Unfortunately, we've seen social-issues fearmongering have consequences that reach far beyond one principal's firing. It's easy to see how this happens: The greater the stakes, the greater the opportunity for the government to convince people to support legislation that strips us of our rights out of fear of some boogeyman "other." Think for a minute about how the stakes are being presented: Republicans in government have convinced large swaths of constituents that, unless you listen to them and agree with what they say to do, your children will be *groomed by pedophiles* who will convince them to *mutilate* themselves, because that's what the Left wants. Conversely, Democrats have so many of their constituents convinced that, unless you listen to them and agree with what they say to do, trans kids will *kill* themselves, and the Right won't even care when they do.

As I hope I've drilled into your brain by now: If someone in government is trying to instill fear in you, the first thing you should do is ask yourself: Why? What do they gain if they're successful? We've already seen fears over Trans Stuff prompt the supposedly small-government, pro–First Amendment conservative Right to support legislation that is clearly anti–First Amendment, like the Tennessee drag ban. The law would have banned "male or female impersonators" from performing anywhere that "could be viewed by a person who is not an adult," if the performance could have been considered "harmful to minors." Now, the Right really kept driving home the idea that this wasn't about adults who enjoyed performing or watching drag, it was just about protecting kids, but think about the implications of a law like this for a second. The

Trump-appointed judge who ultimately struck it down certainly did, reaching the conclusion that it was "chilling constitutionally protected speech." "The chance that an officer could abuse th[e] wide discretion [given for enforcing obscenity laws] is troubling given an art form like drag that some would say purposefully challenges the limits of society's accepted norms," U.S. District Judge Thomas Parker wrote.

He was also, understandably, concerned about how the law applied to anywhere that a child "could" be—because a child could be literally anywhere—as well as the possibility that the law might constitute discrimination—because although it did not mention the word "drag" outright, "the Court cannot escape that 'drag' was the one common thread in all three specific examples of conduct that was considered 'harmful to minors' in the legislative transcript."

I agree with this, and I will take it a step further: The fact that this law was struck down is good for everyone, whether you like drag or not.

"But Kat, this law is specifically against harming kids! Why aren't you against harming kids? Are you a pervert?" Well, I'm glad you asked. Whether I am a pervert is irrelevant to my issue here, which is: In this case, and in so many others, what does and does not "harm" children is subjective. It's up to the individual adult's views on the matter, which also may potentially change based on the child (which is technically anyone from age zero until eighteen), which also may change based on other contexts. The vagueness of a law leaves it open to abuse, and I'm not comfortable leaving my freedom of expression up to the interpretation of government officials.

Of course, some parents are very socially conservative, and those parents might argue that simply seeing a biological man dressed as a woman, regardless of context, *would* be enough to harm children because drag is evil and immoral. If that's already their view, they may think they don't have to worry about the vague language of a law banning gender-bending performances. If drag is an abomination in their minds already, why would they care if the legislation went even further than its alleged intention? But here's why even those super conservative parents should *still* be concerned: the realization that there are other parents who might, for example, believe that *social conservativism* is harmful to children, paving the way for a law such as this to ban people from sharing their socially conservative values anywhere that children "could" be present. The better alternative is to keep the government completely out of determining what kind of art (which drag certainly is) or protest against social norms (which, for some, drag also is) are permitted.

Such considerations played a large part in why Parker ruled the way he did. The standard for what counts as "obscenity" under the law is, as he explained, an "exceptionally high standard as one of its prongs requires that the speech 'not have serious literary, artistic, political, or scientific value.'" That "exceptionally high standard," after all, is not a bug in the system, but a purposeful protection against government power. It is *supposed* to be "exceptionally" difficult for the government to find a reason to ban our speech and expression, and we shouldn't want it any other way.

The bottom line is, it would be far more terrifying for children to grow up in a world where the government has the power to decide what kind of art is or is not permissible than it would be for them to grow up in a world where they might see a dude with lipstick on dancing somewhere. (Make no mistake: This law *could* potentially ban dudes from wearing lipstick in public, depending upon what the government official making the determination believed constituted "harm." Language like "male and female impersonators" and "harm" is so vague, it's indeed possible that anything from an adult trans woman expressing her gender identity to even a Halloween costume might have run afoul of this law, depending on who was making the determination.) We already have laws against obscenity to protect against some of the things that people on the Right seem to be concerned about (yeah . . . legitimate indecent exposure and/ or sexual grooming are already *hella* illegal, if you didn't know), and all of us should agree we do not want to give up our rights to free expression.

Our right to free speech and expression is why I've also taken issue with so much of Florida Gov. Ron DeSantis's legislation. There was H.B. 1557, dubbed the "Don't Say Gay" law by the Left, a characterization that the Right fought by accurately pointing out that the law doesn't even have the word "gay" in it. The actual text of it bans talking about sexuality or gender identity in kindergarten through the third grade in a manner that's inappropriate for children, according to "state standards." What it lacked, however, was specificity on what those "standards" were. By being vague, it left things open to interpretation— and any legislation referring to vague "state standards" when it comes to speech is going to concern me, no matter what the specific subject matter of it is. Even if you agree with what you think Florida's current government's interpretation of this law will be, you should still be concerned about similar powers then being used by a future iteration of its government, with which you may *not* agree.

My commitment to free speech also left me staunchly opposed to DeSantis's "Stop WOKE Act," which banned private businesses and university professors from "instruction" of certain concepts regarding "race, color, national origin, or sex" that ran afoul of the government's ideas about "freedom," such as the idea that whether a person is "privileged or oppressed is necessarily determined by his or her race, color, sex, or national origin." You know . . . "woke" stuff.

Here's the thing: Whether you agree that the ideas that this law would ban are bad ideas or not should not impact how you feel about the law itself. No matter how stupid you think "woke" thought and speech (whatever you consider that to be) is, you have to at least acknowledge that it *is* thought and speech. The state can't banish ideas, and any argument that it should is objectively draconian; I am never going to be comfortable with a politician putting forward legislation that aims to silence certain schools of thought and speech.

If you are fine with it because you happen to agree that "woke" is bad, be careful what you wish for. Similar to my point above: If the government can be used to stop "woke" thought, it could also be used to stop conservative thought. Once you give the government vague, broad powers to control speech based on subjective criteria, any speech is up for silencing. The better move is always to allow for the free exchange of ideas without censorship from the government. (As of the time of this writing, the courts have blocked enforcement of the "Stop WOKE Act" at businesses, colleges, and universities, but it remains intact for K–12 schools.)

So, why then, given all these and so many other examples of illogical reactionary outrage from the Right, did a Gallup Poll released in June 2023 report that social conservatism was at its highest in the United States in almost a decade?

For one thing, the liberals have gone nuts, too.

10

Biology Is Sexist

In the summer of 2023, a United Kingdom–based cancer trust recommended using "bonus hole" or "front hole" instead of "vagina," which was "incorrect language," and might "cause someone to feel hurt or distressed."

Now, as someone who has a vagina (not to brag!) of her own, I can't help but notice how it differs from other holes, including others in the front. For example: Unlike a vagina, a throat isn't supposed to start bleeding, and if it does, you won't be able to solve the problem just by plugging it up with some cotton. Personally? I don't want to call mine a "bonus hole," and I don't know anyone who does. Of course, if I had a person in front of me who wanted me to refer to hers that way, then I would, for all of the reasons I described when discussing pronouns in the previous section.

Use the language you want to use to describe yourself, and I'll respect it; just please show the same respect to me.

Unfortunately? In many cases, in order to be Acceptably Liberal, this isn't good enough.

For many, there's the belief there's no reason anyone might question whether a person who has gone through male puberty would have an advantage over biological women in athletic competitions other than hatred, despite the fact that scientific studies have found, for example, that male puberty "provides a major, ongoing, cumulative, and durable physical advantage in sporting contests by creating larger and stronger bones, greater muscle mass and strength, and higher circulating hemoglobin as well as possible psychological (behavioral) differences," as explained in a 2018 study published in *Endocrine Reviews*, a peer-reviewed academic journal. Regardless of your view on what should happen in terms of policy, you should at least acknowledge that there are reasons some people might oppose biological males competing in women's sports that have nothing to do with transphobia.

In June 2023, the Associated Press officially recommended eliminating the phrase "biological sex," and using "sex assigned at birth," which confused me on multiple fronts: how the phrase "biological sex" could be offensive in any way, and what "sex *assigned* at birth" (emphasis mine) even means. When I googled it, the top definition was by UW Medicine in Washington State, which said: "The sex (male or female) assigned to an infant, most often based on the infant's anatomical and other biological characteristics."

My question for UW? Is it really "most often," or is it always? Because if you really do mean "most often," I gotta hear more about what happened with those less-oftens. It's laughable, really—the doctor isn't *assigning* anything! That sounds like doctors just pick which babies they want to be men and put penises on those babies themselves. What's more ridiculous is that the definitions of "assigned at birth" make it clear that the phrase is really just a more convoluted way of saying "biological sex." In fact, all of the definitions I saw even have the word "biological" in them. If the definition of the new terminology includes the old terminology you're replacing, are you really even replacing anything at all?

And anyway, wasn't the whole point of the phrase "gender identity" that it *was* distinct from biological sex? Or, as *VeryWell Health* puts it: "Sex is biological and based on chromosomes, hormones, and anatomy. Gender is the social and cultural ideas about the roles, behaviors, expressions, and characteristics people associate with men, women, additional genders, or a mixture of genders."

The entire need for a separate category to describe "gender identity"— including, of course, trans identity—is that it, according to its own definition, *is* different from biological sex. So, basically, one could argue that erasing any mention of biological sex actually *erases* trans people. You know, the very thing that might get you canceled today.

Why is no one talking about this?

Unfortunately, it's the same answer for a lot of the issues in this book: The Two Sides have become so polarized, people aren't critically thinking. They're too busy shouting partisan talking points at each other, insisting on showing just how committed they are to their own side, The Good Side, they aren't bothering to consider how we got to the point we're at, let alone how we might start to get along from here.

If liberals were to think about it, they might consider how moving the goalpost from "gender identity is simply how an individual describes himself or herself, regardless of that person's biological sex" to the phrase "biological sex" being in itself offensive might turn some people off, or at the very least, confuse them too much to keep listening.

Could this be a reason for people becoming more reportedly socially conservative, as I mentioned in the previous chapter?

A May 2023 *Washington Post* article covering polling on gender issues reported that "a 57 percent majority of adults said a person's gender is determined from the start, with 43 percent saying it can differ." It also cited a Pew Research study that found "60 percent say a person's gender is determined by their sex assigned at birth, up from 56 percent in 2021 and 54 percent in 2017."

But something that apparently only I noticed was that the authors of the *WaPo* article seem themselves to be confused about what the words and phrases in those polls even mean, writing of another statistic: "Most Americans don't believe it's even possible to be a *gender* that differs from that assigned *at birth*" (emphasis mine), hinting that "gender," not "sex," is what's defined at birth, or that the two terms are somehow interchangeable—again, after so many years of demanding that people understand that they're different!

Another problem with insisting that it's somehow wrong to mention biology is that biology is a necessary part of discussions about social issues. Why? Because biology is sexist.

Regardless of how you identify, and even regardless of what surgeries you might have, there are more than just a few biological and empirical realities that people who were born with vaginas will face that those without them won't.

I had a man I was seeing start calling me Puss Girl, which I initially assumed was a sort of cute, albeit weird, attempt at a nickname. I wish I had left it at that, because when I finally asked why, he brought up my seemingly persistent vagina problems. To be clear— and again not at all to brag, by the way—there is nothing wrong with my vagina, so much as there are so many things that can go "wrong" with any vagina at any time.

When I think about it in context of the gender debate, though? You can identify as a woman, but even if you do, you can't be a Puss Girl if you don't have, well, a puss. But you might be one if:

- You've ever had to visit an urgent care in a strange city because you got a UTI on vacation.
- You've ever brought a Diflucan with you on vacation.
- You've ever worried about being able to pee after sex, and then, once you do, the elation you feel about having been able to pee, thereby possibly avoiding a UTI, brought you far greater joy than anything you experienced during the sex.

- You've ever flipped out over whether your sore boobs were a sign of PMS or early pregnancy.
- You've ever been unable to drink because you were on metronidazole, and then had to try to find a way to explain to the dude telling you that he "drinks on antibiotics all the time!" that the one you're on is different without having to tell him what exactly it is for.
- You started your period early, but unfortunately, not early enough to know that you should not have worn white pants that day.

More than once, I've wanted to walk up to a man and say, "Oh, how much body-and-mind-fucking fake estrogen do *you* have to take to not get pregnant? How do you remember to take it? Or did you opt for the IUD, with an insertion process so painful people routinely pass out during it, because they are fully awake and alert the entire time, because doctors still somehow insist it doesn't hurt that badly?"

The worst thing that can ever happen to a penis is an STD. Sex is inherently, biologically, higher stakes for women—yes, "women" as in Puss Girls—in terms of consequences. Only people with uteruses risk pregnancy, and only people with vaginas risk those far-worse outcomes, like the loss of fertility, in the event that an STD does happen. Having a vagina also means you're risking all kinds of infections that aren't STDs such as UTIs, yeast infections, and bacterial vaginosis—which aren't always due to sex but can certainly be triggered by sex—all things that most women, but few men (or no men, in the case of BV), will ever experience. There's also the orgasm gap; more than 90 percent of men report that they usually have an orgasm during sex, but only about 50 percent of women report the same.

All of this, of course, is compounded by the clear social consequences that women, and only women, face when it comes to sex. No matter how far we have come in terms of women's sexual liberation, it's still true that we don't see too many men worrying about whether to sleep with a woman out of fear that, if he does, she will lose respect for him or never want to see him again. (For what it's worth, I've found a simple way to make this decision, which is to do it if, and only if, at least one of these two things are true: You know for sure that nothing will change between the two of you, or you know for sure that you won't care if it does.)

One of the most sexist things about biology is that women lose their fertility far younger than men do. Like, *decades* earlier. While there are plenty of fortysomething men who will tell you in all seriousness that they're not ready for a relationship, women as young as their mid-to-late twenties start feeling the pressure to find someone to impregnate them ASAP before their eggs dry up. Once they do dry up, they fear, they won't be worth much of anything, except perhaps as a cautionary tale to other women, warning them of the dangers of spending their twenties doing things that make them happy (the horror!) instead of just compromising that happiness to be impregnated by a Bare Minimum Man before they end up over-the-hill-eggless and worthless, too.

I spent most of my life pretty sure that I didn't want kids. Honestly, even at the age I am now—when a pregnancy would qualify as "geriatric"—I still find the idea of it terrifying. Babies are small, fragile, and unbelievably stupid. Whenever I see my friends' babies, I tell them how cute they are, but all I'm really thinking is: *Please do not ask me if I want to hold him.* Like, *hold* a *baby*? When they're that easy to accidentally kill? Did you really just ask me to do that when you just saw me drop my fork onto the floor? And I've had literal decades' worth of experience holding forks!

There are also the fears that some might call "selfish." Like giving up my independence or missing out on opportunities to further the career I've worked so hard to build, especially given my awareness of the empirical reality that mothers, on average, end up giving up far more than fathers do.

Honestly? It's not a popular opinion, but I've always found it so weird that the default response to a pregnancy or even birth announcement is "Congratulations!" when we have no way of knowing whether the kid will grow up to be a serial killer, a drug addict, or someone who uses "*ciao*" as their email sign-off.

Plus, if I dare to muse aloud about possibly of getting pregnant to someone who has already done it, their response usually contains at least a few warnings about how hard it is. *Are you sure you want to do that? It will change your whole life!* It's almost as if they're cautioning me against trying heroin, the only exception being that, unlike a child, heroin addiction is at least possible to reverse.

All of this, and yet I still found myself sitting in a fertility doctor's office with my then-fiancé before my thirty-second birthday, frantically grasping at ways to preserve my own. Even having this option, by the way, was a privilege. It is extremely expensive. A single round of the embryo-freezing process is usually upward of $10,000, not even including storage fees.

It's no walk in the park mentally, physically, or emotionally, either. Either you or someone who loves you enough will have to repeatedly inject hormones into your body at very specific times of day, which will make you feel physically and emotionally *off*, to say the least. (Or, as I texted a friend who asked how I was feeling: "Mentally askew and like my ovaries are going to fall out of my butt.") You have a zillion doctor's appointments and blood draws. You gain weight; I gained seven pounds of straight water weight in just five days. To make matters even worse, you definitely can't blow off any of this steam by working out, because you've been warned that working out might cause your pharmaceutically enlarged ovaries to twist and kill you, and all the while you have no idea whether any of it is going to work.

Thankfully, I was one of the lucky ones. My course was super short, and Cam and I got nine genetically normal frozen embryos out of it.

Many, many women go through this process many, many times and never get nine; many never even get any at all.

As wild as it was, I am super glad I was able to afford to do it, and that it went so well because, as I texted Cam as we were going through it: "I can't imagine how much better I'm going to feel overall when I don't have to hear my biological clock ticking every single moment of every day." Because, yeah, even despite my very clear hesitancy regarding kids, I *still* heard that ticking, especially because it's not like it was just inside my head. There's the biology part, and then there're all the reminders we see when we look around society. I've talked about this before, but it really is worth saying again: "Barely Legal" is a popular porn category; "Barely Fertile" isn't a category at all. All women who want children know that they're automatically faced with an inherent biological imbalance in their romantic relationships with men. We know that we have a much shorter time to find someone to reproduce with than whatever guy is sitting across the table from us, provided that that table is located, you know, anywhere but a hospice. We know. We think about it, and we also know that we can't act like we think about it because of the risk that we'll look desperate.

It drives me insane whenever these Red Pill Influencer types try to rebrand their bullying of women older than thirty as compassion or even as bravery, saying things like, "I'm just letting women know! I'm trying to make sure women know how quickly they have to worry about their fertility; everyone else is too scared to say it, but I'm not!" Like, trust us . . . we know. If you want to be an asshole and make women feel bad—maybe because you've been rejected by a lot of us or for some other reason—just say that. Save us all the time of pretending you're trying to do anything but be hurtful. Oh, and to the women who do this to other women: Has anyone picked you yet?

The challenges that come with XX chromosomes also extend beyond our reproductive systems, which makes me not want to refer to myself using the phrases that some trans activists demand we all use to describe ourselves, such as "people with vaginas."

Some of those are quite consequential: like how males are, on average, physically stronger than females. On average, their upper bodies are 90 percent stronger and have 75 percent more muscle mass than women.

Other stuff is smaller, like the research that shows women work better under warmer temperatures, but office temperatures are usually set to accommodate the cooler temperatures that better suit men. If you bring this up publicly, Men Online will mock you for bringing up something so stupid and claim that you are weak, whiny, and far too sensitive. You may also notice, though, that they will not offer to make any concessions on it themselves. Don't believe me? Try turning the thermostat up two degrees.

So many things come to mind for me, as I am sure is also the case for the women reading this. After all, for us, the statistics I've just listed are far more than statistics. They're personal. When I lived alone in a claptrap apartment in a terrible neighborhood in Long Beach, California, I'd make sure before driving home late at night from the third of my three jobs that I was dressed in men's clothes—baggy sweats, and a baggy hoodie with the hood up over my head—so that anyone who saw me walking from the car alone would think I was a man, which would make him think two things: I was likely more physically strong than a woman, making it more difficult to attack me, and also that I had a dick. It may be transphobic, but it's true: Many rapists are so bigoted that they have a vagina-only genital preference when it comes to their victims.

We should stick together as women—as in Puss Girls—because there really are so many ways in which we can't seem to win. For example: If you're a woman and you're ugly, men don't like you, but if you're *not* ugly, then women don't trust you. (I'm lucky enough to get to experience both . . . I look like Naughty Librarian Barbie after hair and makeup but I look like Garth from *Wayne's World* before hair and makeup.)

When I say "women" there, you know what I mean, too. Yes, there are people born as men who identify as women, and I will refer to them by whatever makes them happy for all the reasons I've already explained. But that doesn't mean we have to, as many activists on the Left might suggest, stop thinking of the word "woman" as "person with a vagina," or that it's wrong to, for example, associate something like a menstrual period with the word. As I so eloquently said in my last book: "[L]ess than 1 percent of Americans currently identify as transgender—which means that the vast, vast, vast majority of people who have ever used a tampon also do identify as women, even if you combine both trans men and cis male frat boys who have soaked them in vodka and shoved them up their asses. No one deserves to be disrespected on the basis of gender identity, but I don't think that acknowledging common associations equals disrespect."

I'm also not any kind of genius for noticing this stuff. Most Americans know about chromosomes because most do make it through at least some grade school. The truth is, if a certain school of thought starts insisting that it's "offensive" to acknowledge what everyone knows to be true, then people might start thinking that it's not a very good school.

Add all of this to the fact that biology rejection isn't even where it ends when seeking to be Acceptably Liberal. You also must accept that there is no age limit for discussing these topics, or even for questioning what a child may say about them, even if what they're saying is that they want to be injected with puberty-blocking hormones.

In April 2022, the *Los Angeles Times* wrote about Erika Anderson, a clinical psychologist who has helped hundreds of teenagers transition, *and a transgender woman herself,* who started becoming worried that all of this has "gone too far . . . that [a] fair number of kids are getting into it because it's trendy," and that some people in the medical system were too hesitant to evaluate those kids' claims before providing hormones or surgeries, in a "haste to be supportive." "The people on the Right and on the Left don't see themselves as extreme," she said. "But those of us who see all the nuance can see that this is a false binary: Let it all happen without a method or don't let any pass. Both are wrong."

Informed and nuanced voices like hers are very important and, unfortunately, just as rare. Just months later, the *New York Times* published an article detailing the "emerging" science on some of the downsides of puberty blockers, "according to reviews of scientific papers and interviews with more than 50 doctors and academic experts around the world," listing potential risks such as *permanent* losses in bone density and fertility—objectively, risks that should not be taken lightly.

And what was the response to that article? Outrage, obviously. From both sides, with many on the Right arguing it was too little too late, and many on the Left arguing that it was (you guessed it!) anti-trans. When each side talks like this, it becomes impossible for us to ever solve anything, get along, or think freely or critically.

Unfortunately, knee-jerk, all-or-nothing partisanship is exactly how most of the conversations go on gender issues.

It's easy to see how this polarization pulls us apart. It makes us assume the worst of each other! Someone who, say, might not want to see certain sexual subjects discussed with young, impressionable kids in schools—especially with the knowledge that these conversations do seem to be having an impact, evidenced by the observations of experts like Anderson, or the statistics such as the fact that the number of students identifying as "nonbinary" in New Jersey schools spiked a staggering 4,000 percent in 2022–23 from 2019–2020—you risk being assumed a conservative on every political issue at best, or a hateful transphobe not worthy of consideration as a human being at worst. On the other hand, a man who enjoys performing in drag risks being assumed to be liberal on every single political issue at best, or a pedophile who aims to sexualize children at worst.

It's sad, but true: Many liberals who read only this chapter would probably accuse me of being a hateful, close-minded TERF. And many conservatives who read only my previous chapter, "Drag Queens Saved My Life," would probably accuse me of being a disgusting, perverted, child-grooming pedophile. If you read them together, though, you will notice that one of them doesn't negate the other. You may find yourself agreeing with more of one and less from the other, or maybe just a few things in one and almost everything in the other. Different individuals who read this section will likely have varying views about varying parts, and that is perfectly okay. For one thing, you don't have to agree with me for me to respect you, and for another? The acknowledgment that we are all capable of nuance—actually beyond capable; it is intrinsic in us as unique individuals—can help us realize that a single point of disagreement on a single issue with a person not only does not render an individual worthless but also doesn't even mean you won't find some areas where you'll agree.

In addition to this division being bad for a society full of individuals who have so much to learn from each other, and where there is so much to gain from community, the level of division portrayed by politicians and the media is simply inaccurate.

Remember that *WaPo* article I referenced earlier? It's a perfect example, because its headline—"Most Americans support anti-trans policies favored by GOP, poll shows"—is rabidly partisan to the point of inaccuracy. On the most basic level, the word "most" inherently means that more than just Republicans must be thinking this stuff, whether your liberal friends will admit it to you at your Prospect Park mommy group or not.

And here's what some of those so-called "anti-trans" policies covered in the polling actually were: "More than 6 in 10 adults . . . said trans girls and women should not be allowed to compete in girls' and women's sports," "[n]early 7 in 10 adults said they oppose allowing children ages 10 to 14 access to medication that stops the body from going through puberty," and "3 in 4 adults said it was inappropriate to discuss trans identity with students in kindergarten through third grade, and nearly as many said the same for fourth and fifth grades."

A majority supported laws forbidding discrimination against trans people in everything from housing to health care to the military and even in K–12 schools. Also, although there *was* that majority opposition to hormones for children, there was also "majority support for gender-affirming counseling or therapy." When it came to the discussion of trans identity in schools: "People were roughly divided when asked about middle-schoolers, and nearly 2 in 3 supported discussion of trans identity in high school."

This article, billed as coverage of division and hate, really detailed just how much people do agree on—most of all, that the issue is nuanced—making its divisive, rage-baiting headline wrong, not only in terms of accuracy but also in terms of impact. It's not zero-sum, after all, to sow unnecessary hostility in our discourse. Just as, say, going out of your way to paint the Left as supporting "groomers" for being no more outraged at videos of a few boobs at a Pride event in the famously avant-garde Washington Square Park than anyone would be about the boobs at Mardi Gras each year (and yes, I did get called a "pedophile" a few times for mentioning this on TV) unnecessarily demonizes a large swath of the population, at the expense of our unity (including unity against government power), so does the Left in attacking the Right for any suggestion that there might be any reason other than homophobia/transphobia for a parent to think it's unfair for their daughter to have to compete against a transgender woman in sports.

Quietly, most people have nuanced views on this very nuanced subject. The way that we are having this conversation currently is simply not doing anyone at all any favors. Actually? That's not true. It has *huge* benefits for one group of people: the government.

Yep. Republicans aren't the only ones who've supported anti-speech legislation based on gender-and-sexuality fearmongering. In fact, in the summer of 2023, Michigan's state legislature passed House Bill 4474, an expansion of hate crime statutes that would make speech that "intimidates another individual" based on things such as gender identity a felony, punishable by up to five years in prison.

The debate over this bill wound up sounding exactly like the one over Florida's so-called "Don't Say Gay Bill," the only difference being that each political party took the opposite side on the Michigan bill as the one they had taken regarding Florida's.

And I mean exactly opposite. Just like liberals had branded Florida's bill as one that might criminalize using the word "gay," conservatives branded Michigan's as one that would make it a felony to not use a trans person's preferred pronouns. In a twist almost too hard to believe, Democrats then defended the Michigan bill the exact same way that Republicans had defended Florida's. Just as conservatives had mocked liberals' concerns over "Don't Say Gay" by pointing out that the word "gay" wasn't even in the bill, liberals now argued against conservatives' concerns by pointing out that the word "pronoun" was not in theirs.

Crazy, right?

As for me, my opinion on this Michigan bill was the same as the one that I'd had about the Florida one: The language is too vague, leaving enforcement up to the whims of government interpretation—a level of power that I am far from comfortable with.

Or, as Michigan state representative Andrew Beeler told *National Review*:

> This entire bill hinges on how you define "intimidation." I'll define it the way the bill defines it: The full definition is, "willful course of conduct involving repeated or continuing harassment of another individual that would cause a reasonable individual to feel terrorized, frightened, or threatened," etc. If you intimidate by that definition, anyone in the protected classes, you are subject to criminal prosecution and a potential felony.

As you may notice, in expressing his concern about the vagueness of the bill from a conservative point of view, he shows why the Left should also be concerned. Think about it: If the person making the decision has a socially conservative view on gender identity, then he might argue that the "repeated" asking for preferred pronouns might represent intimidation, and therefore would be illegal under this law.

To make matters worse, whether the Michigan bill said "pronoun" or not, a survey that came out around the exact same time sure did—one that found that a plurality of millennials, 44 percent, believed that referring to a transgender person by the wrong pronouns should be a criminal offense, with only 31 percent disagreeing. (Interestingly, the number of Gen Z respondents who stated that using the wrong pronouns should be criminalized was less, 33 percent. Overall, the number was 19 percent.)

Anti-speech legislation scares me no matter what side it comes from because of what we would lose if we start giving the government power, *any* power, over our speech and free expression. Again, I wrote a whole book about this stuff, and one thing I touched on was just how backward it seemed that so many calls for laws restricting speech were being presented as somehow beneficial to marginalized groups. I hate to quote myself, but it's not my fault I wrote a book that has lasting relevance. (Wait, it totally *is* my fault; I wrote it!) Anyway, I pointed out in the book that, for "everyone from abolitionists in the antebellum years to gay publications in the mid-20th century, it was free speech and the First Amendment that thwarted the censorship of ideas of a marginalized minority that many people in power considered to be offensive or wrong. When anyone calls for a ban on hate speech, they're assuming that the people in charge of that are going to have the exact same definition of what that means as they do."

Of course, the Left power grabs don't stop at pronoun laws. In June 2023, news broke that New Jersey Gov. Phil Murphy's administration had sued three of the state's school districts for policies that required schools to inform parents if their children showed signs of changing their gender identity.

(To be fair: On the one hand, I kind of do wonder what "signs of changing gender identity" means. Again, I myself do low-key look like a different gender walking out of work in my full hair and makeup than I did walking in, to the point that I have referred to the makeup and clip-in-hair-extensions removal process that is involved in getting ready for bed as "deconstructing my femininity.")

The lawsuit claimed that "'outing' these students against their will poses serious mental health risks" and "threatens physical harm to students."

There's that word again—"harm"! I really can't overstate the importance of people understanding that the word is so completely in the eye of the beholder. While one person might say that a child seeing a drag queen performance constitutes "harm," another might say that what "harm" *really* is would be for a teacher to be legally permitted to mention to a student's parents that their child was showing an interest in drag himself. It is unequivocally and objectively best to leave the government out of making these determinations entirely, because your basic rights should never be up to the sensibilities of whatever government beholder.

Supporting a law like Gov. Murphy's is absurd, and that becomes clear when you take the Gender Stuff out of it. Should any parent *really* be supporting something that demands teachers *deliberately* hide things from parents about their children? To me, that is some unequivocally creepy, communist shit, because the one and only justification at the core of it would be that the state has greater ownership over your children than you do. As I joked when we discussed the issue on *Gutfeld!*, I don't have kids, but I do have a dog, Carl. If I ever went to pick him up from doggie daycare and asked, "How was Carl today?" and they were like, "That's between me and Carl . . . ," I feel like the only reaction that I could possibly have would be something along the lines of, "Ma'am, it sounds like you have an inappropriate relationship with my dog." As for the claim from proponents of this law that sharing that information could lead to a child being abused: Just as there are already laws against indecent exposure and pedophilia—the concerns conservatives cite in justifying laws like the drag ban—there are also already laws banning parents from abusing their children, for gender-identity-related reasons or otherwise.

When you are considering your view on proposed legislation, *especially* if you are very passionate about sexuality and gender issues, the way to the most clarity would be to take the Gender Stuff out of it. This will make it a lot easier for you to look at the nuts and the bolts of the bill and be aware of just what you might be allowing your government to get away with. Don't let them use your own emotions and passions to manipulate you into something you might not truly want.

The same survey that found a plurality of millennials felt that misgendering should be a crime also found that only 17 percent of Americans responded that they would refuse to call a trans woman "she/her" if asked. If you listened to the media, you would think that that number would be closer to the much larger number of people who consider themselves Republicans.

I can admit that, in the past, I have wondered, especially as someone in political media, just why we talk so much about these issues, when trans people make up less than 1 percent of the population. In retrospect, though, the answer seems clear: It's politically advantageous to talk about it. It's a great opportunity for political power players to present themselves as heroes opposite their evil opponents. It not only can use fear to get us to agree with legislation that diminishes our rights, but it also provides one hell of a distraction from other things.

The best thing to do is not fall for it, and instead to do something that we saw people so often shamed for throughout the COVID-19 pandemic: Do your own research. Don't let people with agendas tell you how to feel. Read legislation and varying viewpoints. If you do, you will not only be keen on some of the ways you risk losing your rights but also on how much more we agree on than the people in power over us want us to think.

Don't let the politics of demonization manipulate you into spreading false narratives on behalf of a system that doesn't care about you . . . and maybe, along the way, you'll even find some friends who do.

In Case You Still Like Me,
Let's Talk Religion

The toughest thing about my relationship with my mother, other than the fact that she's dead, is how Catholic she was while she was still alive.

Though, to be fair, it didn't become *that* big of a problem until after I stopped being Catholic myself, which happened within the last eight or so years of her life. And while it would cause some issues before that, many of them were a lot smaller in scale. Like, for example: She would never let me buy short-shorts like all the other girls, no matter how valiantly I'd battled for them in the Kohl's dressing room—fights that got so ruthless they often left me grounded. (Ironically, this meant that the only clothes I was allowed to wear left me looking like a budding little lesbian.) I never got to read any of the Harry Potter books other than the first one, because, after I talked to her about the first one, she became concerned that the se-ries was satanic. A lot of our vacation time was spent doing religious stuff. One summer, we traveled to some sort of Catholic, clergy-run wilderness camp called Companions of Christ the Lamb, where we'd start out our mornings with a religious service and end our nights sleeping on bunks made of plywood. (We did get to go bird-watching in between!)

Every Memorial Day weekend, we'd make a pilgrimage to Carey, Ohio, for a day trip to the Basilica and National Shrine of Our Lady of Consolation. For those of you who went to, like, lake houses on Memorial Day, a typical Shrine Day looked something like this: There'd be church, followed by a trip to the gift shop, where I could get a religious medal or a rosary or something. Later, we'd walk to the park to eat cold meatloaf sandwiches with mustard and play baseball, which I'd find myself *still* completely sucking at no matter *how* much church I was going to, and then participate in a procession through the streets as part of the big group following the clergy as they paraded the Our Lady statue around and led us in praying the Chaplet of Divine Mercy. The leader would pray the first half of the prayers into a megaphone (*"For the sake of His sorrowful passion . . ."*) and we would finish with the second half (*". . . have mercy on us and on the whole world"*), begging God to save us from Hell. After *those* chill vibes, we'd head back inside the church for whatever church stuff we'd missed the other times that we were in there—be that lighting candles and saying prayers or going into the church's basement to look at relics with bones of the saints in them. Then we'd stop at Burger King on the way home, where we'd be allowed to order whatever we wanted, before finally arriving back later in the evening and meeting my father, who (coincidentally, I'm sure) almost always seemed to have too much work to do at home on the day of the trip to join us.

A lot of that stuff could be annoying, but it wasn't all bad. At the time, I was Catholic myself, so the annoyance of having to listen to all my friends' fun stories about riding Jet Skis up north while I had just spent more than seven hours round-trip in a car to go pray and look at bones in a basement was at least balanced by reassuring myself that, unlike them, the way that I'd spent *my* time off would give me bonus points in the afterlife. Speaking of salvation, being kept from the Harry Potter series has at least saved me from becoming one of those weird millennials who keep babbling on and on about how she's a Pufflefluff or a Slitherclaw or whatever, even though she's within striking distance of age forty. (The shorts thing? There was no upside.)

Once I wasn't Catholic, though, my mom's Catholicism became a huge problem—a major sticking point between the two of us that never got resolved. (For the record: I'm not an atheist; I'm agnostic. It's not just that I don't know. It's more that I actually have no idea how I even *should* know. Like . . . me? Have the answers to all the questions of the universe? I can't even parallel park!)

So, why am I talking about religion in this book? Certainly not because I haven't taken on enough controversial subjects already. Definitely not because it's just *such* a party to publicly ponder the most complicated parts of my relationship with my dead mother.

I'm talking about it because, well, I just couldn't justify ignoring it. So much of religion, after all, is rooted in binary thinking. Either you're saved or you're damned. Either it's haram or it isn't. Either you're gonna go to Heaven someday or it's No Heaven Ever.

Now, notice I said "Heaven or No Heaven Ever," instead of "or Hell," because this would ignore that Catholics also believe in Purgatory, a sort of middle ground between the two. It's the place I thought for sure I was going to spend less time in than all my other friends who went to their lake houses for Memorial Day weekend.

The threat of Hell was a major source of conflict between my mother and me. In one such conversation I was home for a visit, and we were sitting at the kitchen table. She was very sick, but I don't think we knew why yet. Doctors told us all sorts of things during that year or so—it was asthma; it was Afib. That mass on her heart was just some scarring from the radiation she'd had during her successful battle with breast cancer six years prior. The summer before she died, they suspected that she might have Stage 4 liver cancer. I remember the feeling of relief we all had when that test came back negative. I'm pretty sure this conversation occurred exactly around that time, the time between our elation in learning that she didn't have cancer and our devastation in learning that it was something much worse—a rare disease called cardiac amyloidosis, a disease that would kill her only a matter of weeks after she was finally formally diagnosed.

Anyway, I remember the conversation a lot better than the specific timing. Just as with all our conversations about religion, it got heated, and left us stuck on the same two sides: She wanted me to believe, and I wanted her to be my mother. I'm not sure exactly what I mean by that, even as I write it, only that it has, at times, meant many different things. Sometimes, I thought of it in terms of the examples I'd seen on television, or among my group of friends, or even in the way she treated my friends, which I felt was with far more leeway than she was willing to give me. I wanted her to tell me everything was going to be okay. I wanted her to tell me that it was fine, and that she fully accepted me and was proud of me and it didn't matter that I didn't share her beliefs. I wanted us to be able to see our relationship as a whole, as mother and daughter. But the conversation was like a malfunctioning camera lens, so stuck on some small, specific thing that it couldn't take in the whole picture.

My questioning usually ran along the lines of: *Mom . . . you love me, right? And you don't think I would deserve to spend the whole rest of eternity suffering in Hell, with no chance of ever getting out, just the way that I am now, right? If you can love me enough to not want that for me, why couldn't God?*

I never did get a real answer. Not from her, and not from Google, either, because, believe me, I've searched for it there, too. Her answer, for the record, was always something along the lines of us not knowing God's plans, or not knowing the details of Heaven's intake process (my phrasing, not hers) after we die.

Oddly enough, my mom's death cemented my lack of belief. Here's a woman who Did Everything Right (at least in the back half of her life—it's my understanding she partied her ass off before becoming my mom). All she wanted was for me to believe. She wanted it so badly, in fact, that as she was receiving Last Rites in her hospital bed, she confidently told the priest that she knew *she* was going to go to Heaven; she was just worried about "them"—"them" being my siblings, my dad, and me—and she wanted him to hear *our* confessions, too.

I often think about what that poor Hospital Priest, a dude whose job already involves talking to dying people about how they're dying, thought about meeting a woman who somehow managed to make that job even harder. I'm serious . . . if you were the priest doing Last Rites at Massachusetts General Hospital in Boston circa November 4, 2014, please, please, *please* reach out to me. I would give anything to talk to you about this. Because, when you tried to push back on her request, she simply told you: "I see an open office right there."

Even more unbelievable? The guy actually did it, and so did we.

When it was my turn, I was honest with him about not really believing in this stuff anymore, but that I was going to go through the motions for her anyway. I don't remember much from the forced confession except for being proud of myself for stopping myself from saying, "You fuckin' *think*?!" after he said, "You seem angry . . ." to me, a person whose mother was about to die much younger than I'd ever imagined she would.

So my logic is this: If a woman *that* devoted to the Sacraments in life doesn't have enough pull in the afterlife to swoop down to Earth and tell her unbelieving daughter that It's All Real, then how could it be real? That's not a joke—I absolutely asked her before she died if she could try to do that for me. I wanted to believe; I really tried to make it happen. Less than a year later, when I heard that the Pope was coming to New York City, I found myself overwhelmed with the feeling that my mom would kill me if she knew the Pope was only a few blocks away from me and I didn't find a way to go see him. Just days before his arrival, I started asking around if anyone was "going to any of the Pope stuff," and, remarkably, my *National Review* colleague Kathryn Jean Lopez invited me to come to the Mass at St. Patrick's Cathedral with her.

I went; I cried. And I mean *cried*. It was a cathartic, cleansing, full-on-intoxicating cry, unlike any other cry I've ever had, and I cry a lot, not to brag. I still think about it sometimes. I've even considered the possibility of attributing it to something supernatural, but ultimately end up deciding that that's probably just what I wish were true, and what must really be true wasn't the work of the supernatural, but of the most basic biological impulse: I wanted my mom.

How could I assuredly attribute my tears to a feeling of her being there with me when they could just as easily be explained by knowing she'll never be there with me again? How do so many other people so confidently have those feelings all the time? Are they only confident in saying that they do? Or is there something I'm missing?

Just two months after my mom died, I moved into that afore-mentioned apartment in Bushwick with a very religious friend as my roommate, who, from here on out, I'll refer to as "Puppet Girl." Well, "from here on out" isn't totally accurate, because that's what I called her back then, too, because she *was* one, and I mean that literally: She was a puppeteer who also made puppets. If that's not a Puppet Girl, then I don't know what is.

Puppet Girl had grown up just blocks away from my own child-hood home, but I didn't get to know her until I decided to do theater my senior year of college. After college, we both wound up in New York City, and, despite our very many differences, we got even closer after that. As we were making arrangements to move in together, the whole Sick Dying Mom Thing obviously came up as well, and when she went back to visit her own family in the midst of it, she took the time to make soup and walk it over to my mom.

She is a devout Christian. I mean, a true believer—she's always been involved in her church, she saved sex for marriage, and she even-tually married a pastor. She's also one of the kindest, least judgmental people I have ever met, and, most importantly of all, did *not* deserve the misfortune of having to live with me, especially during the time that she did. If you recall, my moving in with her was smack-dab in the middle of the brutal six-month stretch of trauma that I wrote about in *You Can't Joke About That*: My mom died, then my grandma died, and then the man I thought I was going to marry broke up with me in front of my dad at Coney Island. The breakup happened just days before I got officially hired at Fox News, and I was putting a lot of pressure on myself to not make anyone at my new job uncomfortable by letting them in on the secret that I was falling apart.

But at home, it's much harder to hide secrets—and the truth is, I was a lost, miserable, dumpster-on-fire disaster. I remember one night in particular, I was so possessed with my own grief that I couldn't stop myself from sobbing and screaming uncontrollably, even though the clock was telling me that my meltdown was a violation of quiet hours. The next morning, when I sheepishly asked her if she'd heard me, she was kind enough to simply say, "Yes, I love you," and get up to give me a hug, instead of saying, "*Obviously* I heard you, you mentally ill banshee; I didn't sleep at all thanks to you." To make matters worse, I was handling the pain by drinking too much too often, and then, to make them even worse than that, attempting to make pasta afterward and failing to clean up properly, resulting in splatters of marinara sauce winding up in confusing places around the apartment.

It must have been so hard to handle, but she handled all of it with love. She told me once, verbatim: "Kat, I just want you to know that I love you so much, even though you're a terrible roommate. My love for you will never die, no matter how much pasta sauce I've had to clean up after you." And she wasn't even being sarcastic! The week that marked the one-year anniversary of my mother's death, I came home surprised to find our refrigerator packed full of my favorite groceries. What's more, I wasn't special; this was how she treated everyone, even strangers. I remember finding her making a list of things she planned to do for *her own birthday*, and it included the tasks: "Buy flowers. Give flowers to someone who looks sad."

Puppet Girl provides a remarkable contrast with the stereotype of religious people as hypocritical or judgmental, and she's far from the only person to have shown me this. For example: My friend Elisha, a devout Christian who helped me edit this book, remains one of my closest friends . . . even though she also knows all the details of the stories I felt were too scandalous to include.

A theme that I apply to politics throughout this book is also true when it comes to religion: Getting caught up in what we think we know about a person based on a single characteristic can leave us misinformed about who that person actually is.

In August 2016, Dr. Kimberly Rios, a psychology professor at Ohio University, and Dr. Ain Simpson, an associate professor of psychology at Miami University, published a study titled "How Do U.S. Christians and Atheists Stereotype One Another's Moral Values?" in *International Journal for the Psychology of Religion*. It found that atheists believed fellow atheists "endorsed fairness/justice values more than Christians," and Christians believed fellow Christians "endorsed all moral values more than atheists," but "both groups held (often extremely) inaccurate stereotypes about the outgroup's values."

The best way to see the good in people with different beliefs is to get to know them better. A Pew study from October 2019 found that "Americans who personally know someone in a religious group different from their own—or who have at least some knowledge about that group—generally are more likely to have positive feelings about members of that group than those who don't."

Honestly, a lot of the hate that I've gotten over my own agnosticism does seem to be rooted in a lack of understanding. The people who attack me over it will act as though my lack of belief is something within my control, or even purposefully defiant, as if the Lord walked up to me, and I told Him to take a hike.

People often aim to convince me of the benefits of religion, as if I am not painfully aware of these myself, but I am. Sometimes, I'll just be washing my hair or walking down the street, and some memory from the past will pop into my head. Then, I'm suddenly hit with the heart-sinking realization that I'll never be that age again; I'm getting older, and to make matters worse, after that, I'm going to die. I'll eventually deteriorate both physically and mentally until I cease to exist at all. I compare this inner turmoil to my memories of my mother, whose belief granted her complete peace as she lay dying. I have far less peace about dying than she did as she was doing it, and I'm not even dying yet. At least I don't think so. At least not except for in the way that all of us technically *are* dying with every moment that goes by, but you know what I mean.

The point is, of course I would rather believe that paradise awaits me after I die. If I could simply choose to believe, as I've so often been screamed at to do, then I would, and I wish people would at least try to understand that before they do the screaming.

But choosing to try to understand others is exactly that: a choice. I know because I've chosen it for myself. I've been given the gift of knowing a lot of different people, including religious ones, and I'm far better for it. I know that a person's religion doesn't automatically mean any host of assumptions about that person must be true. Just as I don't want people to assume things about me because I'm not religious, I don't assume things about people because they are. I treat others the way I want to be treated.

Jesus said something like that, right? From what I've heard, he does seem pretty cool. He hung out with sex workers; he was down to give his friends pedicures or whatever, and his extreme willingness to forgive really resonates with me as a person with some codependency issues.

These are all jokes, of course, but don't get mad at me, because I really do mean it when I say that Jesus had some cool things to say. A lot of the stuff from the Bible is beautiful, and certainly more insightful than the Marilyn Monroe quotes that wind up plastered all over Instagram. (I mean, I've said this before, but I'll say it again: As soon as I read "It's better to be absolutely ridiculous than absolutely boring!" all I hear is "I'm a reckless, sloppy drunk and I might throw up in your car!") I also really mean it when I say that I have close relationships with people who are religious, which has made it easy for me to want to be as kind and accommodating to religious people as I can.

For example: If someone asks me to pray for them, I'll do it, at least the best that I know how. I may not know who or what I'm praying to, or if it even counts as praying if I'm not sure anyone is listening, but I'll still do it. Maybe it counts for something, but even if it doesn't, it's not like it costs anything, either.

You can look at religion and see a rigid binary, yes, but this also offers you an opportunity to look at what kind of nuance can be possible even when such a rigid binary exists. For example: Religion created a very binary rift between my mother and me, but even that was not enough to stop me from having a nuanced view of our relationship, or even of her as a person. Even though it's what I've focused on in this chapter, there was a lot more to her religion than her concerns about Hell. Like Puppet Girl, she really, really cared about people. She was a school social worker, and cared so much more about these kids than her job required, evidenced by the two-day-long viewing at her funeral, packed as a mosh pit full of people with stories about hard things that they couldn't have gotten through without her.

There was also a lot more to her than her religion. She really was like no one I've ever met, and I'm not just saying that because she was my mother.

For one thing, despite being so religious that she kept a St. Benedict medal above every door in our house to keep the devil out and snuck blessed salt into my suitcase whenever I left from a visit home to return to work in New York or D.C. or Los Angeles (as if an unmarked, white, powder-appearing substance in a random little jar *couldn't* have caused me any issues going through security, but thankfully, it never did), she was also extremely crass. She may have been exactly where I get it from. For example, she would always refer to any and every girl in school who bullied me as "what's her tits"—and only as "what's her tits"—from that point forward.

Although her desire to have us all do confession at the hospital may have been due to her deep religiosity, the fact that she was able to convince the priest to actually do it was evidence of something else: Normal social rules just didn't apply to this woman. When I was in high school, the two of us went to a Violent Femmes concert and I lost her. That is, until I felt a kick to the face, looked up, and saw that she, at fifty, was crowd surfing. And she wasn't even drunk! She was a *force*. I hated it at home, yes, but I loved having it on my side against the rest of the world. When I was in trouble in elementary school (which was a lot), she'd always come into the principal's office and terrify everyone with her defense of me. I'll never forget the time she did this for me in the sixth grade, when I got in trouble for finally speaking out about a bully who'd been tormenting me all year.

I was sitting in the principal's office, and my mom came into the office with a folder full of paper, waving it around and saying she had documented evidence of times this girl had hurt her daughter. They were stunned as she told them that she would be taking me home. Later, in the car, she was laughing hysterically. I asked her what was so funny, and she opened the folder and showed me that all of the pages but the first few were blank. She was *that good*, and I really hate that I didn't get to spend more years learning from her how I could be better. Right before she died, I told her I regretted not coming home more, regretted always being away and focusing on work, and she told me: "Katherine, don't be an idiot."

She could be really tough on us sometimes, which could sometimes be really tough on me. She was a very strict parent and kept up her imposing ways even after I grew up and left home. She could be *brutally* critical. I once jumped out of a car she was driving (very, *very* slowly, but still) during an argument about whether the tattooed, womanizing on-and-off-drugs bartender I was dating at the time was a good person for me to be spending my time with. I was barely twenty-two, and the way so many people at that age do, I thought that she just couldn't see what I was seeing, when, really, it was me who was missing things— because, of course, she was right.

No one understood people better than she did; she had a knack for it that I've always envied. I'm pretty sure some of my friends liked her more than they liked me. I'll never forget coming home one Halloween to see her and two of my girlfriends chatting and eating pumpkin seeds at our kitchen table. As a school social worker, she devoted her life to her students. Like I said, her funeral was packed, and I was completely overwhelmed not only by the number of people in attendance but also by the depth of their gratitude for her.

The more I think about it, the surer I am that my mom must have had a nuanced view of our relationship, too. Religious differences or not, she still loved a lot of things about me. On her deathbed, she told me: "Katherine, you were always my favorite sparring partner."

Just as I want others to see my perspective, I've spent a lot of time pondering hers. Looking back at moments like our kitchen table argument, I actually can see why she couldn't just tell me I was fine how I was, and how everything was going to be okay, because, well, in her mind, her oldest daughter was on track to literal eternal damnation, and what could be less okay than that? Although some people, probably especially fellow nonbelievers like myself, might have found her focus on my belief to be unreasonable, I can see how that was not the case based on her beliefs. In her eyes, this *was* love.

I've learned that I don't have to agree with something to accept it.

Being as afraid of Hell as I was when I was religious probably wasn't healthy for me personally, and having the final eight years of our relationship so often dominated by our religious differences wasn't healthy for us. I wish it had been different, but it wasn't, and so now, I just accept that it *was*—and make jokes that, perhaps, what I saw as her granting my friends more acceptance for who they were, I could spin as her caring less whether they went to Hell.

Maybe sometimes, the things that we find impossible to square or place or figure out can show us that not everything has to fit perfectly somewhere for it to just *be*; sometimes, letting something just be is all we can do about it.

I can look at my relationship with my mom in this nuanced way even though we're also on the opposite sides of a binary rift that's far more daunting than religion: the one between the living and the dead. Writing this chapter, I find myself so nervous for it to be published, because I know that I've chosen to share negative things about our relationship, and also that I'm not "supposed" to have done that. As soon as someone dies, they were always perfect when they were alive. *"She was a beautiful, caring, engaging woman."* Sure, all of that's true, but to leave it at that would be to miss so much about her. There are a lot of stories I chose not to share, both bad and good, but I've shared enough to make the point that she was a dynamic person, both good and bad, just like everyone else. Honestly, I think when we hesitate to talk about the imperfections of loved ones who have died, we miss an opportunity to appreciate the flaws in the living. It's true, you never love someone so much as you do when they're gone, but realizing that it was the whole person you loved all along can have a profound impact on the way you view the relationships with the flawed, still-living people around you. After all, as human beings, we're all a bunch of nightmares—and if you think about it, that's kind of what makes us so special.

Conclusion: Hate as a Shelter

". . . hate suits him better than forgiveness. Immersed in hate,
he doesn't have to do anything; he can be paralyzed, and the
rigidity of hatred makes a kind of shelter for him."
—JOHN UPDIKE, *RABBIT RUN*

A little bit of context for this quotation, without spoiling the
book: The main character, Rabbit, has just upset his wife and
mother-in-law in one of the most devastating, difficult, high-tension,
high-pressure situations imaginable and ultimately concludes it's easier to have the women hate him anyway. If they do, they'll leave him
alone. The pressure to help them is off.

If you've made it this far in the book, you already know how common tribal hatred has become and that it's getting worse. As common as
it is, though, it's not like politically motivated volatility changes anyone's
mind. That's obvious, or at least it should be.

Hillary Clinton calling half of Trump supporters "a basket of
deplorables" didn't result in wavering support. Rather, they dug in,
adding the word "Deplorable" in front of their names on Twitter/X.
They didn't make changes, they made *merch*. To this day, you can
buy T-shirts and hats and even a fucking laundry basket on Amazon

that says "PROUD TO BE A DEPLORABLE." To them, Clinton's statement proved she hated them as people, further justifying any hatred they might have toward her. Actually, since they hated her, being hated *by* her was kind of a compliment. A badge of honor! The same thing happened in the reverse when Trump called Clinton a "nasty woman," with Democratic women embracing *that* description and wearing it proudly as their own. I saw a lot of posts on Instagram—often with titties out—with "NASTY WOMAN" as the caption. (Because if there's one thing Trump hates, it's definitely boobs!)

So, if it doesn't change anyone's mind, what's the point? For politicians, it's easy to see what they gain. I've explained these benefits repeatedly throughout this book: There's no better way to motivate people to get out there and vote for you than if the other option is not simply inferior, but actually evil. Plus, as it did with Rabbit, the hatred here quite literally keeps them from having to do anything. If your supporters believe the Other Side is irredeemable, then what is there really to do? Work *with* those pieces of shit? Why do that when you could just do nothing and blame them for the problem instead? Plus, if a problem never gets solved, that's a win for you, too. After all, as long as a problem remains, you'll get to keep using it to keep your political power. You won't even have to update your talking points!

And hatred can be a shelter for us, too. For one thing, it protects us from taking the kind of good, hard looks at ourselves that make us feel bad. When a girl's boyfriend breaks up with her, her friends will often tell her, "He's a loser!" and "He sucks!" and "I never thought he was cute!" Why? I mean, in my case, the friends saying that to me were often just being accurate, but there are other reasons too: By making the dude look like less of a prize, the girl gets to feel better about herself when she's feeling down, and the girl's friends know that. It's much easier to tell yourself that your boyfriend broke up with you because he was too immature for a real relationship than it is to confront the fact that maybe, for example, you *shouldn't* have gotten blackout drunk at his work party and cornered his boss to talk to him about how ready you are for a baby and *What are the company's options for paternity leave?* when you've only been seeing each other for three months. (No, I didn't do this. But I can see how you might have thought that; it's not like I've never acted crazy. One time, when a guy blocked me, I kept sending him $1 on Venmo—using the "What's it for?" section to tell him how I was feeling and that we should get back together. The good news? It worked. The bad news? It worked.)

Much like acknowledging that someone who broke up with you might have had a reason for doing so, it can be hard to acknowledge that the other political team might have some good points or, at the very least, good *intentions*.

If you believe the other party is evil, then you get to be good simply because you're against them. If all Democrats are groomers, then you're not just a Republican; you're a warrior protecting the innocence of children. If all Republicans are racist, then you're not just a Democrat; you're a modern-day Rosa Parks. If opposing views become just opposing views, though—and not manifestations of immorality—then your views also become just views, and not manifestations of morality. If you accept that Republicans aren't bad just by the very nature of being Republican, then you'll also have to accept that being a Democrat doesn't automatically make you a better person than everyone who isn't.

But the truth is, the only thing most of the people viewing themselves in these inflated ways might have in common with Rosa Parks is that they're sitting on their asses. The difference, of course, is that their ass-sitting is *not* a heroic act—no matter how much people seemed to act like it was during COVID. My God, was it ever easier to signify yourself as One of the Good Ones than it was during COVID? By doing nothing (as in, literally nothing, sitting at home on your couch all day and night), you were saving the world. People who wanted to open their businesses to feed their families were bad, and you, an ass-sitter, were good, simply because you *were* an ass-sitter. Incredible! Really, it's no wonder some people seemed to never want it to end.

Now, I'll concede that a predisposition toward tribalism exists in the wiring of our brains. A July 2023 article in *Psychology Today* discussed this phenomenon, citing a bunch of different studies from a bunch of different neuroscientists about how belonging to a group or tribe—and interacting with others seen as a part of our group—activates all kinds of different rewards systems in our brains, motivating us toward those kinds of connections to get those good feelings.

Now, no offense to all those people in that article who spent a lot of time and money becoming neuroscientists, but I didn't need to be a neuroscientist to know that. People will behave in some truly insane ways to feel a sense of belonging.

As that neuroscientist-sourced *Psychology Today* article pointed out, bonding with the members of our group can spike oxytocin, the bonding chemical in our brains—but "oxytocin can [also] contribute to bias, leading to favoritism toward one's own group," also pointing to research showing that our brains can create a "heightened emotional response to out-group members." Humans crave connection, and, unfortunately, a common hatred absolutely can provide a means of connection. Just look at the shit you and your friends talk about other people in your group chats! (If you don't know what I'm talking about, then, uh . . . I've got some bad news for you.)

Clearly, this whole dynamic is having an impact on us in terms of our politics. In October 2020, Jocelyn Kiley of Pew told NPR that nearly 80 percent of Americans claimed to have either no or "just a few" friends on the Other Side. Which makes sense! Again, even neuroscientists say that this sort of arrangement is a natural inclination.

So, in a lot of ways, hate *is* easier. If you assume everyone from the other political party is irredeemable, that this or that problem is this or that group's fault, then—just like in the case of Rabbit—the pressure to be any sort of help to solve anything is off.

But just because something is your natural inclination doesn't mean that it's what's best for you. Getting up before work to run to nowhere on an elliptical machine, for example, is not what I'm naturally inclined to do, but I logically know that I need to do some kind of cardio sometimes to combat the stress that my clinical anxiety and nicotine gum habit must have on my heart. So, knowing that it goes against your natural inclination to venture outside of your own tribe shouldn't be an excuse not to do it, but a reason to realize that you're going to have to actively work to break out of it.

And you *should* want to break out of it! Closing yourself off from people who think differently from you will make you more susceptible to believing incorrect assumptions about them, leaving you with a less informed view of the world than you might have otherwise. And that's only one of the many disadvantages: As cultural scientist Alana Conner writes in an article in *Psychology Today*, "research shows again and again that grappling with diverse opinions and backgrounds makes us better decision makers, more creative problem solvers, and more empathic people."

So, even though it's tough—and in many ways, unnatural—refusing to try to get along with other people who disagree with you is not a good thing. That's true not only for the sake of society, because we'd all be better off if we could get along and come together to solve our problems, but it's also in your own individual self-interest. You could be limiting your creativity; you could be limiting your support system. You could be preventing yourself from meaningful relationships by writing people off unnecessarily based on your false assumptions about them.

The good news is also the scariest and most stressful: If we want things to change, it's up to us.

The best place to start is to just try. To do what I've been saying throughout this book: Open yourself up to people whom you've closed yourself off from, and approach conversations with people who think differently with more curiosity than judgment. It also helps to focus on what we have in common. Think back to that study I mentioned in the "Politically Nonbinary" chapter, for example, the one that found that about 9 out of 10 Democrats and Republicans agreed on the importance of core values such as compassion, fairness, and personal responsibility.

Another key, I think, is also what I've been doing throughout this book: being willing to be vulnerable. I've shared a lot of deeply personal things about myself, even embarrassing stuff, and I've done so on purpose. After all—unlike the times that I've horrified myself by oversharing at parties—the writing and editing process involved with publishing a book would make it impossible for me to have shared any of it just impulsively. I've had to decide over and over again that, yes, I am sure I want to talk about my abusive ex, about my struggles with my mental health, about my sexuality, about my insecurities, and about the difficulties in my relationship with my now-dead mother.

I'm not perfect; I don't have it all figured out, and there have been times in my life that have been messy. But guess what? No matter who you are, I'd bet that it's the same for you. We all have our dark times and our shortcomings and our fears. I know that it can be scary to admit those things (believe me, I've lived that fear every single day waiting for this book to come out), but approaching a conversation with the attitude that you know you're not perfect makes it a lot more likely that the conversation will be productive and meaningful. It's tough, but it's true: If you want people to see you as a human being, then you have to show them that you are one.

So, ultimately, Rabbit's point about hatred is true: When we are "immersed in hatred," we "don't have to do anything." The problem, of course, is that also means we'll miss out on doing anything *good*.

Acknowledgments

Thank you first of all to Simon & Schuster for believing in this book. A special thanks to my editor, Natasha Simons; my agents, Anthony Mattero and Mark McGrath; and my manager, Matt Beales, for all of their hard work and hustle in getting this out there.

To Fox News! To Suzanne Scott, and to Greg, Tom O'Connor, and everyone else on the *Gutfeld!* team for providing me with a platform to speak my mind freely and to have fun doing it.

Another special thanks to my husband, Cam, who is the actual most patient man in the whole entire world. Thank you for being cool with me having papers strewn around our entire living space during edits, and especially for assuring me of your unconditional support during my many bouts of all-encompassing panic about putting myself out there like this . . . I could never have done it without you. I love you more than words can even describe, and I'm pretty good with words.

To my family: Dad Timpf, my brother, Elliott, and my sister, Julia. To my dead mom, Anne Marie Ochab Timpf. It's been nearly ten years without you, but your influence on me as a strong, outspoken woman is evident on every page. I wish you could see this, even though I'm sure you'd certainly have some words for me about some of it.

To the boys, Cheens and Carl . . . who actually, now that I think about it, provide one hell of an argument for the possibility of total opposites to be able to live together (at least mostly) peacefully.

A huge thanks to everyone who read this book ahead of time and offered their advice. A very special thanks to Elisha Maldonado for her brilliant editing work. Your ability to aid me in reining in my prose is perhaps surpassed only by your ability to rein me in emotionally.

Thank you to everyone I dated in my twenties! I don't know where I'd be without the content you provided me.

Finally, thank you so, so much to all of the friends throughout my life who have refused to allow political differences to stop us from being friends. I love you and let's hang out soon please.